DR. JAN COOPER

CONVERSATIONS
—— WITH AN ——
ANGEL

A Parable for Today's Time

This book is written to provide information and motivation to readers. Its purpose is not to render any type of psychological, legal, or professional advice of any kind. The content is the sole opinion and expression of the author, and not necessarily that of the publisher.

Copyright © 2025 by Dr. Jan Cooper.

All rights reserved. No part of this book may be reproduced, transmitted, or distributed in any form by any means, including, but not limited to, recording, photocopying, or taking screenshots of parts of the book, without prior written permission from the author or the publisher. Brief quotations for noncommercial purposes, such as book reviews, permitted by Fair Use of the U.S. Copyright Law, are allowed without written permissions, as long as such quotations do not cause damage to the book's commercial value. For permissions, write to the publisher, whose address is stated below.

Printed in the United States of America.

ISBN 978-1-64552-289-8 (Paperback)
ISBN 978-1-64552-291-1 (Hardback)
ISBN 978-1-64552-290-4 (Digital)

Lettra Press books may be ordered through booksellers or by contacting:

Lettra Press LLC
30 N Gould St. Suite 4753
Sheridan, WY 82801
1 307-200-3414 | info@lettrapress.com
www.lettrapress.com

CONTENTS

Introduction xi
The Journey 1
The Conditioning 7
The Torment of the Early Years 13
A Special Mission 21
The Findings 32
The Findings 39
Declaration of the World 48
Argument with an Angel 55
Dream Speech 62
The Great Hall 69
The Signing of the Declaration of the World 81
The Race for Peace: Training 87
The Race for Peace: The Starting Gun 92
The Run toward the Finish Line 100
Miracles Are Coming Your Way 104
Testimony 106
About the Author 111

To all women, men, and children who are sincerely interested in improving themselves, their lives, their families, and their world in *peaceful* endeavors.

I want you to know God has a plan for your life. It is a plan of good not evil. It will give you hope and a future. You are special. You are as precious as a jewel, like a lump of coal you have been developing your skills and talents that are now at the level of a diamond! You have dreams! God put those dreams in your mind, but they will only happen if you act upon them. Action is the key to anything real or imagined! An American renaissance is in the making, and artists and crafts people are preparing for our rebirth. A rebirth that will unite you with what God has called you to do. Only you know what that is.

GOD HAS PLANS FOR YOU!

My newest CREATION has been a 50 year journey "CONVERSATIONS WITH AN ANGEL!" I pray you will enjoy it, as much as I enjoyed CREATING it for you! Be PERSISTENT and everything will come to you at the right time.

INTRODUCTION

Over Two Thousand years ago God sent his Son JESUS Christ to earth. He was a perfect man who overcame the world and suffered on the cross to save us from our sins.

During World War II, he sent another son with the initials JC. He did not overcome the world but his fears, insecurities, guilt, and self-doubt have left him. You can do all things through Christ who strengthens you. I pray this little book will help you, as the Holy Spirit has helped me to write it.

"He that walketh with wise men shall be wise; but a companion of fools shall be destroyed" (Proverbs 13:20).

You become known by the companions you keep. If you associate with men of wealth and knowledge you will be considered *wise* and *learned*! If you associate with liars, cheats, and drunks, that too will be your *reputation*!

You are your own artist! You are your own brushes! You are your own colors! You are the star of your life! *Turn your life into a masterpiece*!

"Hear counsel, and receive instruction, that thou may be wise in the latter days" (Proverbs 19:20).

I want you to know God has a plan for your life. It is a plan of good not evil. It will give you *hope* and a *future*. You are special! You are as precious as a jewel, like a lump of coal you have been developing your skills and talents that are *now* at the level of a diamond! You have *dreams*! God put those *dreams* into your mind. But they will only happen if you act upon them.

"Let your light so shine before men, that they may see your good works, and glorify your Father which is in Heaven" (Matthews 5:16).

Whatever your talents may be, let them be of such a high quality that all men will know that your creations were to honor and glorify our Father which art in Heaven, giving Him all the credit.

Action is the key to anything real or imagined! An American Renaissance is in the making and artists and crafts people are preparing for our *rebirth*! A rebirth that will unite you with what God has called you to do. Only you know what that is.

"David ran away and escaped" (1 Samuel 19:10).

You too must escape if you want a new you. You must invest in yourself and your future and pay off all debts *ASAP*.

THE JOURNEY

Once upon a time, that time being the beginning of World War II, a baby boy was born on the steps of a white hospital in a small town in Kansas. This baby boy—his name was Winston—never knew his father. His father was killed at Pearl Harbor.

Three years after Winston's debut on the planet and his father's exit from it, his mother married another military man. As a part of a military family, the boy traveled from state to state, school to school, and country to country. He grew up lonely. Never in one spot for long, he hesitated to make friends. In fact, he did not know how.

One midsummer evening when the boy was sixteen, he took a walk on a narrow path adjacent to the runway not far from the base housing. He was crying. As he kicked rocks and pebbles to the side of the path, he talked to himself. He talked also to God, whom he considered his best friend. As he walked, the air became strangely chilled and breezy for a midsummer night.

"God, I thought you loved everyone. If you love us so much, how come life is so hard? I've been lonely all my life. I'm fat. I get bad grades in school. Whatever side of the tracks I stand on is the wrong side. And it's not just me that feels the pain. It's all over the place. My family travels a lot, and there's no place that seems much better. I've seen people living in poverty. I've seen people who are prejudiced against other people. I've seen people hurting each other. Millions, many of them innocent, languish in prisons. It's all so unfair!

"If you really do exist, Father, please help me. At least let me know that you're there. Give me a sign. Give the world a sign."

The weather began to change even more rapidly. The moon turned the color of burgundy wine and started to spin slowly, like a precious stone being examined by a jeweler.

"Father, I'm trying to believe. Is this you talking to me? I'm trying to listen."

The wind hummed through the branches, and Winston was sure he heard a deep whispering voice talking to him.

"You are not alone," it said into his ear. "Through your pain, you have been conditioned since birth. You will do great things someday. You have been prepared for your destiny, as your son and his son after him will be." The wind rose in pitch, and the boy grew chilled.

The voice began to fade, and Winston walked home slowly. The loneliness moved in again with the silence. At home, he closed his bedroom door and cried.

In heaven, the Father was summoning an angel to Himself. Though he could slice through galaxies at immeasurable speed, this angel took his time. His was a leisurely flight. He paused at a planet to watch the sun rise over its edge and butter its atmosphere with pale yellow. The color reminded him of the gold of heaven, and he continued on his way, musing that some humans no longer believed that heaven's walls were gold embellished with jasper, sapphire, topaz, chalcedony, emerald, aquamarine, amethyst, and a host of other precious gems. He had always suspected that the Father had buried such treasures in the ground on the planets to remind those who looked down of the shimmering clarity of the heavens.

"The heavens," he spoke aloud. "Heavens! I've been summoned, and here I am dilly-dallying," He continued his flight with more haste.

The glow in the distance became the colored sparkling of the heavenly walls, which gave way to the white sheen of the pearls that covered the twelve gates. As the angel swiftly approached, the gates began to tremble and clatter. Startled, the angel stopped and hovered outside.

"Father? Is that you?"

"Do not be afraid."

"But why do you meet me at the gates? Have I offended?"

"No, good servant. Our business demands haste."

"What is it, Most Loving One?"

"It is time for your sending and another's receiving. Two rivers must join and flow together for a time, one heavenly and one of the planets. You are the one."

"And the one I shall visit?"

"He is an inhabitant of one of the planets that still tolerates disharmony."

"Which planet?"

"Go now. Make haste."

"But, Father—"

"Trust your wings, worrisome one. They will take you where you need to be."

"Father—"

"Does the river inquire of the sea? It simply flows according to its own nature and thereby arrives. Do likewise. Go now."

So the angel prepared himself. He coated his wings with Borazon lest the journey be long and chafe them. He closed his eyes and let himself be. He turned to the left with a mysterious assurance and began to fly. In his mind's eye, he saw a blue planet girded with white clouds. Still deep in space, he heard the faint clamor of frantic lives of that planet. He veered toward a small star and watched as it grew to fill his vision. Closing in, he glanced to the side, and there it was, the blue planet. Now inside the star's solar system, he paused in an orbiting belt of asteroids and dust. His vision and hearing penetrated the clouds around the planet, and a shocking display of earthly reality assaulted his heavenly mind.

Sifting through the grunts of life from the surface, he heard the angry shouts of nations and the explosions of war. He felt the disharmony, and tears began to run down his cheeks.

He saw rockets being launched into orbit and across imaginary borders on the planet's land masses. He watched as families split apart. He saw murder, theft, and a host of other perverted acts all across the planet. He could see truth scattered among the lies, but most overlooked it. Just as he was about to shake his head and fly on, he heard a familiar voice above the din. It was God's voice. Here and there he was speaking quietly to many people. Some listened. Some spoke aloud of what they heard and were ridiculed or sent to institutions by those who did not believe them.

Others ran from the voice of God. Some ran back to their day-to-day ruts. A few heard only a little of what the Father said and tried to turn it into power to quench their greed and bring them wealth. When they gained nothing, they reached for more. Others ran into the fog of alcohol and drugs where they tried to hide. The angel saw that many chose the wrong path out of fear of the truth. Exhausted, the angel began to doze off. The meteor against which he had been leaning suddenly rolled out of its orbit, startling him awake, and began to plunge into the earth's atmosphere. The angel hung on for the ride until the meteor burned itself out in the upper atmosphere.

Up close, the planet was the color of milk and honey. The angel began to circle it in a slow flight.

From his position, he could see how many people had trouble balancing their lives. He saw homeless people using the sides of buildings and curbs for urinals. He saw the broken bottles, colored shards so unlike the gems of heaven, marking the slide into despair. He saw these wandering ones begging for nickels and dimes, eating their meager meals under store awnings. Below the gruff shells that they had grown to protect themselves, the angel saw their cuts and bruises and their inner scars.

Needing to rest his mind, the angel flew back into space, leaving behind the clamor of broken lives. He did one somersault after another. He abandoned himself completely, executing dives, flips, and rolls. Refreshed and knowing there was much to accomplish, he soared down to a drifting cloud, paused, and reached up to the glowing aura that was his halo. He passed a finger through its golden light, causing it to pulse and quiver. He called it "adjusting his halo." A quick series of sparks, like stars, raced around his head, and the halo began picking up the signals of the planet's media.

Again he began to fly across the planet. He heard radio announcers speak of robberies, rapes, price increases, murders, child abuse, and wars. Ghostly images of knives and guns and fires and angry arrests floated before him. As he circled the globe, the languages changed, but the stories remained disturbingly similar. As he listened and watched, his sensitive angel hair began to streak with gray, and his brow became wet with perspiration.

"Father!" cried the angel. "I am of the spirit, not of the flesh. What can I do about all of this but listen and cry? I think you have sent me here to ease their way, but I do not know how." He wept heavenly tears. "I am of the spirit, not of the flesh!"

"The spirit is deeper than you know, wet-cheeked one!" replied the heavenly parent from out of the din. "Search your inner depths. Trust your heavenly instincts. You will find your direction there."

"Father, there are so many people crying and in need of help. How can I choose one to visit?"

"The choice has already been made. Flow like the river to the sea. Trust your nature."

The angel adjusted his halo again to work like radar, sensitizing him to shapes and movements as he flew in closer to find the one he was to help. He hovered over hills and mountainsides, through valleys and canyons, cities and towns, roads and trails, beaches and blacktop. He saw so many people content to live the way they were, concerned only for their own personal pleasures and whims.

"So many are crying," he muttered to himself. "I don't know how to help them. I don't know who to help. I'll fly around the earth one more time."

Like bees swarming over honey, the multitudes filled their days with frantic activity. The angel wondered if they might, underneath it all, really be trying to make their worlds better. Still the sound of crying continued. The angel glided past the coastline of Europe and felt the cool air of the Atlantic Ocean below him. He swooped left and then right again, unsure why except that it felt natural to do so. Within seconds, he found himself outside a military housing complex in the Southeastern United States. His halo crackled and went silent, returning to a soft glow. A window seemed to beckon him, and through it, he saw a boy on his knees.

THE CONDITIONING

Winston lay with his head on his pillow, his face streaked with tears. A bright glow outside his window caught his eye. He sat upright. Very clearly, he saw a face outside his window surrounded by a glowing aura. The image astounded him, though for some reason he was not afraid.

Seeing the astonishment on the boy's face, the angel suddenly realized how foreign he must look. He ducked back away from the window, and with a wave of his hand he transformed himself. The glow of his halo became a ruddy glow on his face. His wings disappeared, and street clothing covered his body.

Then the angel materialized in the boy's room. Winston, mesmerized, watched every move the angel made. The angel walked across the room and took a piece of bubblegum from the top of the dresser. He unwrapped it and popped it into his mouth as he picked up a yo-yo.

"Wow, this gum tastes good. It's been a long time."

"You could have asked."

"I'm sorry," replied the angel, a little taken aback. "I forget about the old concept of ownership. See, where I'm from—"

"Everybody shares, and everybody's happy, and nobody is selfish, and nobody owns anything," the boy rattled off in a singsongy, sarcastic voice.

"Exactly."

"Yeah, right. Where did you learn to do 'around the world'? I mean since you probably don 'I' *own* a yo-yo?"

"You're quick. I like that."

"So where'd you learn?" repeated the boy.

"Oh, around," said the angel with a smile.

"The world?"

"Something like that. I know that you have to trust your instincts and just go for it, let the yo-yo fly," countered the angel as he blew a bubble. As Winston watched fascinated, the bubble grew big enough to block the angel's view and then popped onto his glowing face. Startled, the angel lost concentration and the swinging yo-yo hit him on the head. Winston laughed for the first time in days.

"Why don't you tell me what's the matter?" asked the angel, suddenly serious.

"You have gum on your face."

"Better than egg."

"I like you. You're funny."

"Tell me," insisted the angel.

"I don't know."

"Sure you do. Start with the things that are on your mind right now. That's always a good clue."

"Why should I? Nobody really cares what I'm feeling."

"I do. That's why I'm here. This gum sure loses its flavor fast."

"That's what you get for trying to taste it with your eyebrows. Who are you?"

"I'm here to help you with your conditioning."

The boy looked startled. "How did you know about that?" he asked.

"I heard his voice too," said the angel, relieved that the tiresome listening had paid off.

"The voice in the wind was real?" inquired the boy tentatively.

"His voice is as real as He is."

"Who?"

"Our Creator. Our Heavenly Father. God."

"Right, and I suppose you're my guardian angel?"

"Yup."

"Nice to meet you. I'm the Boy Wonder, able to leap tall bubblegum-faced lunatics in a single bound!" The boy stood on his bed and lifted his arm as if brandishing a sword. "Able to conquer all he attempts!"

"Your words are more accurate than your thoughts."

"About lunatics?" teased the boy.

"About conquering what you attempt," answered the angel seriously.

"Angels don't wear jeans. Where are your wings?"

"You should listen to your words." The angel continued. "You become what you think."

"Right. Look, I'm your dog! *Arf! Rowf! Rowf! Arf! Arf!*" Winston began bouncing on the bed with one arm curled under his armpit. "I'm your chimpanzee! Oo-oo-oo. Ah-ah!"

"I hid them."

The boy stopped. "What?"

"The wings. I hid them. Or rather you did. It's not what you expected. Not what you thought. The jeans are."

"What are you saying, that I created you from my thoughts? Can I make you do tricks?"

The angel waved his arm where his halo had been. With a snapping sound, he went sparks and tiny globes spinning about the room.

"Whoa!" exclaimed the boy with open mouth. "How did you know? How did you do that?"

The angel replied softly as the sparks faded, "You create your own angels or your own devils with your thoughts." He stepped toward the dresser. "Mind if I have another piece of gum?"

"You mean I can help myself?"

"It's your gum."

"Not to the gum. I mean, *help myself.*"

The boy sat cross-legged on the foot of the bed as the angel came closer.

"Who else?"

"If that's true, then people all over the world can heal their own hurts. People can make things more peaceful and happy."

"You're pretty smart. You are already speaking words of wisdom." A different kind of tear rolled down the angel's cheek as he imagined the wisdom spreading out from this young boy. "So young."

"What?"

"Nothing."

The boy stood and began bouncing on the bed again. "Want to act like an ape?" he asked in innocent invitation.

"There isn't time. You must begin to learn to help yourself. Faith will help you."

"Faith?" asked the boy, genuinely puzzled.

"Faith," replied the angel. "The thing that created me. Your belief."

"Where do I begin?"

"Examine your own existence. Examine the world around you. Pay attention to what is happening on the planet," the angel instructed.

"I already do that. In a way. But I need help."

"I will help you. But you will have to do all the work."

"What do you mean?"

"You must examine yourself. I cannot do that for you. You must observe the happenings on the planet through your own eyes. Then you must list your findings in order to draw some conclusions."

"That sounds like school. I can't! That's just like in school. Everyone knows I can't! Even my dad calls me a 'dumb shit', and Mom always asks me why I can't be like the other kids. My French teacher said I'm too dumb to graduate. I can't! I'm fat and dumb, and

I have no friends. I can't. I can't. And you must be pretty dumb if you don't know that. Some angel you are!"

"You are listening to voices that are not your own, little wise one who lapses." With those words the angel began to draw letters on the ceiling. "Listen to your own voice. It knows better than the others who you are." The letters on the ceiling spelled "You can" in glowing gold.

Winston had always expected the answers he sought to be given to him. The prospect of having to search and figure things out left him feeling anxious and afraid. Afraid of failure. The responsibility of his quest overwhelmed him, and he began to cry.

"Crying is good, my new young friend," said the angel, as he began to dematerialize and fade.

"Don't leave me! Why can't you just tell me the answers?"

The angel replied in a voice as thin as his dissipating appearance, "Answers unsought are answers unheard and unremembered. Seek." With one thinning translucent wing, he reached over and wiped the boy's tears.

"I'm just a kid, for crying out loud!"

"And I'm just an angel."

"What's your name?"

"Tavett," he replied as he ascended through the ceiling. "Tavett Tobert."

He was gone.

Winston slammed his fist on the mattress in frustration and cried, "I'm only a boy."

Tavett's head popped back through the ceiling. "Our Father knows that! Sheesh!"

Winston giggled and threw a pillow at the ceiling. In silence again, he wept quietly.

THE TORMENT OF THE EARLY YEARS

Winston lay with his head on his pillow, his face streaked with tears. A bright glow outside his window caught his eye. He sat upright. Very clearly, he saw a face outside his window surrounded by a glowing aura. The image astounded him, though for some reason he was not afraid. Thus began Winston's period of self- examination, a critical period in his life that lasted nearly forty years. Rather than simply living his life, reacting occasionally to the highs and lows, Winston began to examine the events in his life. Meeting an angel had convinced him that his life had meaning. He set out to discover what that meaning was. His was not a methodical search, as if there were a Holy Grail to find. His was a search for meaning and truth and not so clear cut.

The journey was a little chaotic for a young boy. His mind became a jumble of questions, prayers, and observations. The angel watched Winston from afar, waiting for the time when he would again be needed.

One evening when he saw the boy mutter something to himself, the angel grew curious. He tuned into the thoughts swirling around in the boy's mind. What he heard was typical of the churning ocean of consciousness that daily and nightly filled Winston's head:

"Why? Why? Why am I always afraid of failing? Because you fail at everything you do, that's why! Why am I always failing? Why do the other kids make fun of me? How come they never accept me?

Why did Walter hate me enough to hit me, turning my eye purple? Why did I hate him back for a while? I hate to hate! Why did I want revenge? Am I just like Walter? Yuck!

"No, I'm worse. I'm fat. I hate school. I hate my parents. I hate the whole damned world with its mean people. Why was I even born? All I ever wanted was to be normal, to be good at something. Is that too much to ask? I just want somebody to care about me. Is that so tough, God?

"God. Yeah, right. Why do I even bother? If there was a God, would He let the world be so messed up? Huh? What you have to say for yourself, God? It's not a pretty sight down here. Why did you make me the way I am? Why couldn't you have made me good at something? Just one little thing, is that too much to ask? So change me. It could be a sign. Then I'd believe in you for sure. I hate being a failure.

"School is stupid! How am I supposed to learn anything when the teachers are just like my parents? They make me feel about three inches tall, just like good old Mom and Dad.

"The stars are bright tonight. How can they be so bright when everything else is so dark? I don't like brightness. I like that blue fog that circles around me on the inside. It's calm. Very, very calm. I wish the world would just be quiet.

"Did you hear me, world? Shut up! Why can't you just leave me alone? It's like the world hates to leave someone alone to think. It hunts the quiet ones down and pounces on them and screams in their ears! I should just leave. Get out. Leave the country. Tomorrow.

"But the world's nosy and noisy everywhere! We're all trapped!

"I'm not listening! La la-la-la-la-la-la-la-la-la-la-la-la-la! Shut up! Stop chattering! How many different ways can the world say nothing? Nothing. Nada. Zippo. I'm leaving.

"To where? People are cruel everywhere. Just when you start dreaming about some other country, you turn on the news and hear that they're starting a civil war, or some terrorists have attacked another country. People are so sick! Maladjusted: learned that one in school today. Not in vocabulary. Miss Williams called Albert that. Maladjusted. To what? This world? Being adjusted to this world, now that's maladjusted.

"Nobody helps anybody. People would rather kill you than help you. That stinks. Like dead things stink.

"Has anybody figured this mess out? God, probably. But He's keeping it all to Himself.

"I'm not really as bad as I sound, God. Lots of times I really believe in you. I try not to have hope. Try to talk myself out of it. But it's no good. If I really thought it was all a waste of time, I wouldn't get so mad. Or so sad. There you go again, Winston, saying the 's' word. I hate it when I cry. Salty and wet and stupid.

"Okay, I admit it. I do believe people can be good to each other. I believe I can. I just need the strength. God? Please give me the courage to fight the meanness. Inside me and outside me. Please? Help me keep believing what I believe, no matter what anybody else says. No matter what happens in the world.

"So why would God answer you, Winston? Why are you so special? Who am I anyway? Am I really being prepared for something like that angel said? Sometimes that angel just seems like a crazy kid's dream. But it seemed so real. Still does. Why can't I just give up? That would be easy. Why do I keep trying? Is it you, God?

"My head hurts. Big thoughts, little brain. Hurts then goes numb. Then the ringing. Stop already! Please stop.

"We're all going to die if this doesn't stop. Bombs. Wars. Injustice. Depression. Torture. Fried liver. It's getting crazier and crazier every day. We have to all sit down calmly and figure this out before it's too late.

"People were born to think. Better than fighting. Fists don't make anything better, but minds do. At least they can. People make fun of the intellectuals, but they're the good guys. Just look where the fighters got us!

"Nuclear bombs! It's pretty hard to talk it out with a nuclear missile pointed at your head. It's hard to do anything. Why did we make something that can destroy us, the makers? That's pretty stupid. Let's make something whose sole purpose is to unmake us. Dumb. Really dumb.

"Maybe, God, if you let us all see what's in store for us, we'd be more careful. You know, people want to believe in you, even if it seems they don't. It's just so hard when you seem to be so silent all the time. Please help me learn more so I can help people, give them confidence that they can make things better. If kids could see the good inside themselves, if they could be encouraged, they would end up creating angels instead of devils.

"Angels. Devils. Bombs. It's like we live in some weird dream. Living in a dream. A nightmare. Who's running this place anyway? Us? Politicians and dictators? God? Is there anyone in charge? We've made so little progress. Where does the evil come from? Man is the evil in the world. How can mankind be the hope if it's the evil too? My head hurts. Oh no, the dizziness again. The lights. My eyes are sore from the tears.

"At least I have a goal. At least I'm trying to understand. Enlightenment. It's like a yo-yo. You rise and rise, and things seem to make sense, and then you start to ask even more questions, and you realize that the questions are infinite in number, and compared to infinity you know almost nothing, and then you go down. But realizing that you have so much to learn is a major thing to learn, and the yo-yo starts back up again, spinning all the while. You learn and then you learn how much you have to learn. Up. Down. Up. Down. Spin.

"I like yo-yos. Thank you, life.

"The yo-yo. Is that why people accomplish things and still see themselves as worthless? They accomplish something and then see how much there is yet to be done? God, please help us work to our potential and then be happy about it. Help us see the undone things as adventures for tomorrow. Help us be happy with ourselves.

"Why is it that just asking questions makes me feel so much stronger than I ever did? Is it because questions open possibilities? Yeah. Asking a question is like opening a door. You wouldn't ask if you didn't believe an answer was coming! That's it! Asking a question is an act of faith! You have faith that answer exists!" He felt giddiness come over him.

"I never used to ask questions." He giggled. "I just made statements to myself. Mostly I repeated the negative statements other people made about me. They were like locked doors. No possibilities. No escape from the judgments. But my questions are my own. They're positive. I have to remember to stay away from the negative old statements if I'm going to grow strong. Confident. Grow proud. Grow in love.

"I am seeing so much more than I used to. Where do these thoughts come from? You, God? For years, I had no confidence at all. I didn't know how much I could learn just by focusing on the possibilities.

"Sometimes I see new ideas like colors in a marble. They're real. They're beautiful. But I can't quite touch them. I can't get them out and chew on them like the insides of a walnut. They're just there.

"God, if you are the source of all the color, of truth, then I want to serve you. I want to be an instrument of yours to help more people find the pathways to peace.

"I can see it now. I'll be God's servant. I'll grow happier and happier as I grow older. I'll help people see the truth, and those people will help other people see, and the ones they help will help others. Different races and religions will learn to love each other. Problems will be solved because people—men, women and children—will be opening the doors to possibilities. All over there world, there will be peace. Love will spread like clover. People will join hands, just happy to be alive. People won't just buy the Bible; they'll read it. Artists and musicians will celebrate the rebirth of humanity. The hands of God will unfold, and His voice will be loud enough to hear.

"But how can humans be the hope if they are the evil in the world? How can it all get better if some people refuse to learn? What will happen to those who always demand what they think they want?

"Man is the evil in the world. That's a statement. A judgment. A closed door. I used to believe that. What's the open door? A question. 'What is man that you should be mindful of him?' That's a question in the Bible. What is man? A question. An open door. What are the possibilities for man? What is man? Man is his possibilities. We make of ourselves what we are. We have the possibility of being loving, peaceful builders of bridges.

"We have to stop putting our energies into meaningless things: closed doors and rigid judgments. If we make statements about each other, we can believe them without ever talking. We never have to check to see if they're true. We can make war because of those statements. But if we ask questions of each other, we have to talk, interact. You can't question someone and make war on him at the same time.

"Question. Seek. 'Seek and ye shall find.' That's it! Keep searching for truth and there won't be time for hating. There won't be enough energy. We won't kill what we want to get to know. Other people. Or ourselves. Start with ourselves. If we seek and find ourselves, we will like it so much we will want to know more, to know others. We will take care of humanity because we want to know humanity.

"Father, God, I can feel you feeding my thoughts. I like it. I like what I'm thinking. But it's all coming so fast. I'm thinking faster than I can understand. Be patient, if I forget. I'm slow sometimes. Sometimes I'm afraid.

"Fear. Men and women run from each other, from love, because they are afraid. But love is the most important thing. Love is holy. We love what we know. Like that old blanket I have. It's not the prettiest. It's torn; it's stained, but I love it. The more I use it and know it, the more I love it. Love is an open door.

"Fear is a closed door. It has already decided without seeking. It thinks it already knows what it will find. It doesn't ask because it assumes it knows the answer. Question fear, and it will crumble because it doesn't really know what it thinks it knows. Question fear the way you test the black shadows in your room at night by turning on the light. The monster in the closet was just a bathrobe. That's funny in the light. Question fear, and you'll laugh at it. Seek and ye shall not be afraid.

"Stop! Please, God, stop! It's too much. My head is beginning to hurt again. Even good thoughts can make your head hurt! Please slow down. I feel like I'm in a wagon with no brakes on a steep hill. Let me rest!

"Please don't be mad at me. I'm just being honest. I'm only mostly a kid still. These are big thoughts for a kid, you know. Solomon was old when he wrote about wisdom. Well, older than me, anyway.

"Why is wisdom so hard to find? Why can't I just sit and listen in a classroom or find it in an old box in the closet? Sheesh! This is work. Brain jogging. Homework from heaven. Ease up a minute, okay?

"God?

"I believe. In you. In peace. You taught me to ask. You opened the doors. I can feel myself rising, standing. I'm not so different from anyone else. That means other people can rise above the fear and pain too. The possibilities. Thanks. Can I rest now?"

Tears that the angel did not see rolled down Winston's face. They were gentle, silent tears. They shimmered with the colors of the marble. Opalescent tears of quiet joy.

Winston was born anew. Winston became a questioner. Winston was a seeker. To seek became his lifeblood.

This much the angel knew. He smiled.

A SPECIAL MISSION

Forty springs and summers passed, and the boy became a man with responsibilities, a wife, Sandi, and a son, Michael. Winston grew in knowledge and insight, but in many ways wisdom still eluded him. Wisdom is a connected thing. Knowledge applied. Winston's knowledge stayed on the inside, detached from his words and actions, like water trapped in a pond with no outlet. The stagnation that set in became conflict, conflict with his son.

One week before his high school graduation, Michael, carrying a painting and a small brochure, interrupted Winston in his book-lined den and business office.

"Dad, can we talk for a minute?"

"I'm very busy right now, son," Winston replied, taking his feet down from the desk, recognizing that his stance and his answer did not mesh. "Can't this wait until tomorrow?"

"You'll be just as busy tomorrow. You're always busy. It'll take only a minute," replied the boy. He held up the painting for his father to see. Winston did not notice.

"Come in. Have a seat. What can I do for you?"

"Stop treating me like a business client, for one thing," Michael answered in frustration.

"Don't be difficult, son. I'm very busy." "So you said."

"What did you want?"

"There's a small school I want to go to in the fall."

"You can go to any school you want, as long as it offers what you want: finance, law, or engineering. But I'm telling you, if you go to a school with a name, your chances of success are better."

"That depends on what you consider success."

"What's that supposed to mean?"

"Dad, I don't want to study engineering or law. And I definitely don't want to study business."

"You can do well with business. Look at me."

"Yeah."

"Well, what do you want to study? Medicine?"

"You really don't know, do you?" Michael said with a hint of pity in his voice.

"I'm not a mind reader."

"Dad, it doesn't take a psychic! I'm sitting here with a canvas beside me."

"So?"

"Dad, I want to be an artist!"

"No!" thundered Winston.

"What do you mean, no?" asked Michael, exasperated.

"No means no. Do you want me to throw your educational finances away so that you can be a starving, homeless artist?"

"Thanks for the vote of confidence."

"Mike, I know you can draw, and that's a nice hobby. It's just not a living. Artists starve. They become famous only when they're dead! It makes them crazy. They're kooks. They don't live up to their responsibilities. Is that how I raised you?"

"What do you mean how you raised me? When did you do that? I surely didn't notice! Was that on your lunch breaks? Or was that in the evenings when you were yelling at Mom? Or maybe that was what you were doing when you stuck your head around the corner and said to be quiet because you had an important call. Is that what that was, raising me? Thanks for telling me. I never knew!"

Winston met Michael's passionate gaze with his own steely one. In a deliberately quiet voice, he said, "I think that will be quite enough. Your time is up, young man."

"Got an important phone call coming in?" Michael answered, his voice thick with sarcasm.

"I run this business for you. What do you think puts the clothes on your back and food on the table?"

"Oh, no, you don't! You can't hang this on me! I never chose to be your kid. I never asked to sit at your table. You do this for you! You get off on the power. You like all that fame and money! This is not about me, this is about you. You don't even know me!"

"What are you talking about?"

"I'm an artist, Dad! I'm one of those kooks you talk about. You see this canvas? This is me! And you didn't even see it!" Tears of frustration welled in Michael's eyes. He fought them back.

"I know what's best for my own son!"

"You don't know anything except this damned business! I swear to God if an angel flew in your window, you'd offer him a cup of coffee and start talking budgets and timelines."

Father and son stood glaring at each other. Michael's last words hung in the air between them. Something stirred in Winston's chest.

He felt for a moment that he was a teenager again, looking into a mirror. Something about his son's passion was so familiar. He thought of angels. His mind flashed on bubblegum and yo-yos. He forced himself back to the present. An instant had passed. The glare continued. Something inside, something cool and peaceful swelled up. He took a strained breath.

"Only if he had references."

"What?" Michael was caught off guard.

"And his wings weren't from some endangered species. Too much potential for costly litigation."

The smile began tentatively. Michael saw it and tried to recapture his punctured anger. He began to chuckle instead. The chuckle became a laugh, and in a moment father and son were teary-eyed with laughter, bent over desk and canvas.

"You're a sick man, Dad!"

"I'm not the only one seeing angels."

"I told you. I'm an artist."

"Are angels bondable? I have to know."

More laughter. Tension, years in the making, forced itself out into their mirth. As it slowed again to chuckles, and then subsided, a silence took its place. The tears in Winston's eyes did not subside along with the laughter. He looked again at Michael.

"Son," he whispered. "I'm so sorry."

He was surprised at the strength of Michael's arms. It had been too long since they had hugged. His shirt felt warm and damp, and his nose ran. They eventually pulled apart and stood a little awkwardly.

"So tell me about this college. We'll need to make arrangements quick since you'll be away in Europe this summer."

"Thanks, Dad."

"Is this school accredited?"

"Fully. Dad?"

"What?"

"About the Europe trip . . ."

"What about it?"

"I told my friend Jack that I'd lend him my graduation money for his first semester of college."

"What!"

"His parents can't afford to send him to college, and he won't have enough from his summer job to pay his expenses. He's already got a job lined up at school, but that doesn't start until September. He's been accepted to one of the best science departments in the state, but they won't hold a place for him until the spring semester. He has to go now, or he may not get in."

"We gave you that money for Europe."

"Jack's college is more important. I'll go to Europe when he pays me back."

"*If* he pays you back."

"My friends don't lie."

"Money changes things."

"Like it did you?"

"That was uncalled for."

"I'm just trying to help a friend."

"With my money!"

"Oh, now it's your money again? I thought you gave it to me."

"For Europe."

"So what does that mean, that anything you give me is only mine if I do what you want me to do? I decide to help a friend, and you take the money back? What about my clothes? Are they mine? No wait. I'm going to be an artist. I guess I better give them back."

Michael removed one of his shoes and threw it across the room.

"There! There's your shoe back, Daddy! I might drip some paint on it. And here's the other one. You want my shirt too?" he asked as he tore at the buttons.

"Stop it!" demanded Winston. "You're acting crazy."

"I'm an artist, remember? I'm supposed to act crazy."

"If you think I'm going to pay for your art school after this—"

"I don't expect anything from you! Your word doesn't mean anything. You give things only on conditions. Shoes. Money. Love. You used to talk about God. You told me to believe, to share. Now when I do, you call it crazy!"

"I can't afford to help the whole world!"

"Tell it to God!"

"People have to learn to fend for themselves."

"I suppose nobody ever helped you when you needed it? I thought you'd be proud of my helping Jack. You're such a hypocrite! You disgust me!"

Michael grabbed the painting and threw it at the wall, hitting the bookshelves and causing a rain of books.

"What do you think you're doing?" shouted Winston, still stinging from his son's words.

"Sharing my soul with you! Enjoy it. Thank you for your valuable time."

The door rattled the wall when it slammed shut. Winston did not question the events that had just transpired. Instead, he poured himself a drink. He picked up one of the fallen books and wandered over to the couch to read. It was a book on great philosophers. Reading philosophy worked like a sedative for him. He began to doze. Philosophers stepped one by one off the page and into the room of his mind.

Pascal smiled indulgently at Winston and held up his right index finger. "We owe a great debt to those who point to our faults, for they humiliate us. They prepare us for the exercise of correction and freedom from guilt."

Winston tried to object, but his lips would not move. He tried to ask a question but could not. He saw the closed doors across the room. He thought he saw his son.

"Truth is too simple for us. We do not like those who unmask our illusions." It was Emerson who had spoken.

"Don't leave out God, Mr. Emerson," chided MacDonald. The man turned to Winston and continued in a soothing voice. "I want to help you grow as beautiful as God meant you to be when he first thought of you."

"That is a good wish for the man, sir, for to be what we are and to become what we are capable of becoming is the only aim in life."

"Ah, but, Spinoza, sir, in order to be what we were meant to be, we must have eyes to see what we are." Thoreau joined the group from the pages of the book. "We must contemplate, dream. If you have built castles in the air, your work need not be lost. That is where they should be. Now put foundations under them." He cast a probing glance at Winston, who suddenly remembered the knowledge he had worked so hard to gain and then hid in his mind.

"I said, *wake up*! We have work to do. Come on, Winston!" Winston yawned and rubbed his eyes. When he opened them, he saw a vaguely familiar face framed by a pair of plush white wings.

"This dream is getting more interesting by the minute. Ouch! What was that for?"

"Aren't you supposed to pinch someone who thinks he's dreaming? I heard that somewhere."

"You!"

"Ah, the light dawns!"

"You're that dream I had as a kid. The angel."

"*Shh!*"

"What?"

"Be quiet a second and listen to the beating of your heart."

"Why?"

"Just do it."

Winston listened. The deep thumping in his chest was soothing. He began to genuinely relax and listen. He heard a door click open. He heard the wind in the trees. He heard a voice. Startled, he looked at the angel.

"You're real."

"Ta-daaaa!"

"You haven't aged a bit, you still look the same."

"You treated your son badly. He's been conditioned, too, you know. You could learn some things from him. He could learn from you."

"It was just a spat."

"You know, Winston, if you would only apply some of the things you figured out through the years, you might be an okay guy. Today was not okay."

"I remember. I didn't always understand the things you told me before, but I remembered them."

"Even if you didn't apply them. You promised our Creator that you would serve Him and other people." The angel picked up one of the boy's shoes. "From what I see here, you seem to be slipping. What's in the glass?"

"Brandy."

"If I drank this stuff, I'd be eating asteroids every time I fly! Be careful with this."

"I've managed."

"To what? Become a success in the world's eyes? You have a bigger mission. Or have you forgotten?"

"Not forgotten, so much as set aside. I guess making money felt natural. And safe."

"It's not too late."

"What do I do?"

"Think about your son, your family, your neighbors, your Creator. Remember the people who have helped you."

"And then what?"

"Does the river inquire of the sea? No. It simply flows according to its own nature and thereby arrives. Do likewise. Go now."

Winston hurried to his desk and pulled out a small leather-bound object. He ran to the door, opened it, and shouted into the house. "Where's that kooky artist son of mine?" He scribbled with a pen.

"Dad?"

"Come here, son." Winston was giggling like a kid. Michael approached cautiously. "Here. Take this."

"What is it?"

"It's a check, what do you think?"

"For what?"

"Jack's first semester of college. And it's not a loan. It's Jack's graduation gift."

Michael smiled. "He's not your kid."

"Says who? Artificial distinctions, my boy. You should know that. You're the artist."

"Thanks, Dad."

"Not bad for an old hypocrite, huh?"

"Yeah, not bad."

"Now go tell your mother to go shopping for some travel clothes. But tell her to check the weather forecast in Tahiti first."

"What?"

"Well, you don't think we're going to sit around twiddling our thumbs while you and Jack are in Europe, do you?"

"Me and Jack...?"

"Your mother once told me she would renew our wedding vows only if I flew her to Tahiti, so—"

"Mom!" shouted the boy. "Dad's completely lost his mind, and if you bring him to his senses, I'll never forgive you."

Father and son stared at each other with laughing eyes. Winston whispered, "Not a chance!"

Winston took an extended leave from his work, his first break in five years. He sent the servants home on paid vacations. He painted the house and weeded the garden. He spoke to friends on the phone. He gave free advice over the fence to his neighbors on business and community involvement. He cooked meals with his wife, Sandi. He spent hours talking to Sandi and Michael, together and separately. He marveled at the similarities between his son's goals and dreams and his own. They talked together of world peace. "Ya done good, Winston!"

Startled, Winston turned to the corner of his room from which the voice seemed to come. There stood a jeans-clad angel playing with a yo-yo and popping his gum. His broad grin showed teeth that shined like opal. "Real good."

THE FINDINGS

"Remember years ago when I asked you to examine your existence, observe the happenings in the world, and then list your observations and conclusions?" The angel Tavett was balanced on the back of the couch in Winston's study. Winston had moved his office out of the house so that his time at home wasn't spent working.

"Vaguely," replied Winston.

"Vaguely?"

"Hardly at all."

"Is that why you have all those lists written down in those old diaries?" asked Tavett. "Do you vaguely remember those? Those diaries with a last entry from yesterday?"

"Why do you ask me questions if you already know the answers? Pretending to be mortal?"

"How else can I carry on a conversation with a mortal?" the angel queried. "Besides, I'm modeling for you, showing you how to keep asking questions."

"I wish you wouldn't balance on the back of the couch like that. It's so…otherworldly. Couldn't you just sit in a chair like a normal heavenly being?"

"Now who's trying to get me to act human?" Tavett slipped into the seat of the couch and folded his hands with a staid expression.

"You look like Whistler's Mother."

"Was she human?" Tavett asked.

"Ask Whistler."

"Show me your findings, Winston. You'll need them when you meet with your friends and associates."

"Most of it is borrowed from great thinkers, Tavett. I mostly put their ideas into my own words and tried to apply them to my experiences in the world."

"Good. That's the beginning of wisdom," Tavett noted. "Applying great ideas to your experiences is how you make them your own. Until then, they are just theories. Show me."

"Four decades, and I've got only a half dozen pages or so."

"Wisdom doesn't have to be wordy," Tavett said.

Winston handed a worn diary to the angel. He opened it and began reading in a sonorous voice.

"These things I hold true:

1. A wise one is not afraid to break the barriers of the past.
2. Those who fear rejection will shun closeness and thereby create what they fear.
3. Only by admitting faults can one overcome them and begin to grow.
4. Accept people as they are, and you will find love. Try to change them, and you will love an illusion.
5. Only when a man knows his needs can he pursue prosperity.
6. He who serves up a banquet of criticism will one day be forced to eat the same meal.

7. It is good to offer a helping hand to those in need, but true help comes when I teach others the strength of their own hands. Offering my hand should be my first act. Teaching them the freedom of their own power should be my second. This applies to countries as well as individuals.

8. True bravery is working for what you believe in.

9. When you find you are in error, it is best to admit to it gracefully. Those who do not will be found out and look the fool.

10. Boredom is caused by energies channeled in the wrong direction.

11. The boss wants to be God, but God chooses not to be boss.

12. In order to believe, one must first seek.

13. No matter how small, commitment is the seed to a happier life.

14. Negative criticism is the worst of enemies. It turns men into defeatists, women into dependents, and children into rebels.

15. If a beneficial word is offered in a positive tone, others will listen and try again. This is a power everyone has.

16. The wise man works for someone who allows him to think. The fool becomes a vegetable in someone else's garden.

17. Too much discipline creates robots who cry themselves into rust." "Well?" "Well what?" the angel asked. "Do you like what you're reading? Is it good?" "Am I your judge?" "No, but you're a friend. I value your opinion, and I think I can learn from it." "I think there is much that is true here," Tavett commented. "I hope the Father will help me help you reach your full potential in applying these truths, understanding them in context. You know, turning truth into wisdom."

18. "Finding a common language is a key to diplomacy between all to share one. Talking can prevent wars.

19. Every action matters—successes or errors—for through action we learn.

20. Everything a person encounters in life is necessary to make that person who he or she is now.

21. Everyone can learn from everyone.

22. Friendship is a difficult gem to mine. Extract it slowly and then cherish it like a family heirloom.

23. A true friend will encourage you to have other friends.

24. Feelings are like steam: hold them in too long and something will have to explode or crack and leak.

25. Failure describes an action, not a person. A person never loses the potential to succeed.

26. If you would succeed, know yourself and thereby your path.

27. Whatever doesn't flow stagnates. Whatever doesn't grow degenerates.

28. The hardest thing on the planet to know is yourself.

29. All people suffer loneliness. It cannot be filled by taking from others, but only by giving of oneself.

30. Though it is difficult, love is possible. Those who would find love must continue to give of themselves. Many have missed love only because they gave up trying.

31. When walking down the marriage aisle, the wise one walks slowly with both eyes open.

32. Every highway has a map. It is the fool who refuses to unfold it.

33. Every man and woman is an island, and every woman and man is a master bridge builder. If we desire to connect, we can.

34. What is a nation but people with the same feelings, hopes, and desires? No nation is above another.

35. The machines we have created are hungry. If we feed them truth, we will reap the benefits of peace.

36. The only realities that exist today are the ones we allow to exist." "This is better than I thought it would be," said the angel, looking at Winston with a new respect. "Thanks, I think. I just kept asking questions like you told me to." "Must have been some good questions." "Honest ones. That's the only kind that counts," replied Winston casually. "I see your wisdom is becoming second nature to you. Nothing is impossible for those who believe," Tavett offered. "In order to believe, one must first seek," Winston said. "I read that somewhere." "Me, too." Smiled the angel. He looked back at the diary and continued.

37. "People pay more attention to the surface plant than to the roots that reveal its secrets.

38. Respecting yourself is the beginning of growth.

39. Respect every man, woman, and child regardless of their actions, and often you will teach them to respect themselves.

40. Share what you know with others, and they will share with you. To learn, you must be generous with knowledge. This is true of nations as well.

41. There is power beyond physical strength. Brain strength grows with time; old people are often the strongest. Listen to age.

42. School does not teach about life. Only life can teach about life.

43. All questions are good questions; they are the mind opening doors. All questions deserve answers and respect.

44. The attuning that society needs is not by artificial means.

45. There is natural truth in the universe. Complex problems come from ignoring simple truths. This applies to people and to nations.

46. Only those who have accepted the concept of a Creator can know what is best for them."

"You have learned more than I thought you would," commented the angel as he laid the book on the coffee table. "What is the most important thing you learned?"

"Is this a test?" Winston asked.

"Just a question," Tavett said, smiling. "You forget, we're not so into judging where I come from."

"I learned that most people look to the future for things to be better," Winston said. "They expect their children's lives to be happier than theirs were. They don't want their children to make the same painful mistakes, and yet they are not really willing to admit when they do something wrong. How can things get better if we ignore the problem of human wrongdoing? The best thing they can give their children is the simple statement, 'I did wrong, and I'm sorry.'"

"You have much to share with others, Winston. Try to find a way to organize your thoughts. Your findings are jumbled right now. If you organize your knowledge, it will be easier for others to understand. You will be able to teach people about living in harmony and peace. Keep learning from the great thinkers of the past."

"There are so many. It takes so much time! Isn't what I have enough?"

"It's a good start," said Tavett, "but not enough to fulfill your mission. Wisdom does not rush into the room like a teenager to the phone. It takes its time. You Earth dwellers expect instant results. All good things take time and patience. I'm going to go now. It's time you arranged a meeting with your friends."

"Don't go yet, Tavett. Tavett? Tavett?"

THE FINDINGS

Winston fell asleep on the couch in his den. He dreamed high dreams, dreams of making the world a little more peaceful. In one dream, he saw history like a river. He watched it at its source, bubbling from the ground. He watched history flow down through the ages. It became a powerful river, full, surging forward until it came to his den. There it began to pool and threatened to inundate the house. It had no outlet. Startled awake, Winston realized that he had lifted his legs to avoid the rising water from his dream. Feeling foolish, he lowered his feet to the carpeted floor.

Upon waking fully, Winston made arrangements by phone to visit with several friends who lived throughout the world. Most were pals since boyhood. To accommodate his busy schedule, they agreed to meet in a reserved room at the airport of the midsize city where they all grew up.

On the appointed day, Winston flew in on his private jet. He entered the room and greeted his friends warmly. They received him graciously and emotionally.

Winston looked around at this old friends assembled and said, "I should never have let so much time elapse without seeing you all. It's great to see you!"

"You look pretty good, Winnie, coming in your own Learjet! Mr. Big Shot," replied Girardo, a tall, ruggedly handsome man who looked as if he would be as comfortable in a lumber camp as in a city. He was the owner of a popular local bar and pool hall.

"Mackie" McEntire, the mischievous one of the group growing up, spoke next, "What have you been up to, Winnie?"

Oggie, always wanting to know the angle, added quickly, "Yeah and what's this little get-together for?"

"I had a visit with a good friend who reminded me about how important friendship is," Winston replied. "That's something I've been neglecting."

"This mean you're going to stop by now and then for a game of pool?" Smiled Girardo.

"I was hoping for more than that, Girardo," answered Winston.

"Hey, I'm not that kind a guy." Girardo laughed. "Seriously, man, we've been reading about you in the papers. You're pretty important. What can we offer a guy like you except a couple of beers and some laughs?"

Oggie bent over Winston's sleeve. "Wow! Would you look at these cuff links! And this suit, must be three, maybe four hundred dollars."

"Oggie, stop sniffing the money, it's embarrassing," Ira finally spoke after sitting aback for a time and observing. Ira always seemed to be assessing any situation. Oggie stepped back, and Winston looked sheepish. "Don't mind, Oggie. The rest of us realize you didn't dress to impress us. You probably don't own a pair of jeans."

"The friend who sends me here does. Sort of"

Ira continued, "I read you've moved up in the bank again. Before long, you'll be single-handedly setting interest rates for the whole world."

"I'm not quite that important. The press is good for the bank, though."

"You make it sound like you're a lowly clerk," injected Girardo. He picked up a bowl of peanuts from the table. "International banking isn't peanuts. Peanut?"

"I've shelled a few nuts in my time," answered Winston, reaching for the bowl.

"Yeah, I remember. What was her name?"

"Oggie, you have a knack for reducing everything to its lowest denominator." Chortled Ira.

"That can be a valuable asset. Most of us spend our time covering the basics instead of seeking them," said Winston.

"I just find it a little crude at times."

McEntire turned to Ira smiling. "And that's bad?"

"You wouldn't know the definition of bad," retorted Ira.

"Mackie *is* the definition of bad." Laughed Girardo, as he playfully punched the arm of his old friend, McEntire.

Winston shelled a peanut and held up the nut between his thumb and forefinger. "This is why I am here."

"Peanuts?" asked Oggie.

"No, stupid. It's a metaphor. Big bankers never say what they mean straight out," chided McEntire.

"That's one of the reasons I need you guys," said Winston, almost to himself.

"So what's it mean, then, smarty-pants?"

Winston poured water for each of them and replied, "I'm here to talk about the possibilities for making things more fruitful."

"You're going into farming, Winnie?" Ira asked with a raised eyebrow.

"I'm talking about the world, about people. If we could help make the world a more peaceful place, we'd make it a more productive place socially and spiritually."

"I think this is over my head," said Oggie, reaching for a peanut. "It just looks like a peanut to me."

"Shouldn't you be talking to the Vatican or at least congress?" replied Ira.

"I'm just a small businessman with a pool hall," added Girardo.

"You own the old place now, Girardo? I didn't know that. I thought we were still managing it. Congratulations! Geez! I remember sneaking in there when we were kids." Winston sat musing for a moment and then continued, "It was ordinary people who brought about the birth of the greatest country this world has ever seen. It's ordinary people who make the real changes. Just regular people learning to recognize what they really need, what's good for them."

"I've sold a lot of things in my lifetime," injected McEntire, "but I'm not sure how peace will play in Peoria."

"It's possible because it's what people really want underneath it all. Girardo, do you think we could use the hall to meet, say, maybe once a month?"

"What are we, the five apostles?" snorted Oggie.

"Oggie, if you could wish one thing for the world, what would it be?"

"Free cable television for everyone!"

"Seriously, Oggie, seriously. What?"

Oggie looked intently, almost defiantly, at Winston. In the silence that followed, his gruff expression softened. Finally, he whispered softly, "Peace," and dropped his eyes to the floor.

"Girardo?"

"Peace."

"Mackie?"

"Peace. Definitely peace."

"Ira?"

"Peace, of course. But that's not the point. What can we here in this room do except dream of world peace?"

"That's where it begins," answered Winston with excitement in his voice. "We dream, we question, we believe, and before you know it, even Oggie can't deny that it's real. Name me one great change in the world that didn't begin with a few dreamers willing to act on their dreams? I know you guys. It's been a long time since we've been together, but we knew each other back when we weren't afraid to dream, to believe. Those dreaming boys are still there underneath all the protections, maybe, but they're still there. I can see it in your eyes."

"Are you confusing naivete with wisdom?" challenged Ira. "Look around you. The streets are filled with violence. How do you talk peace to the barrel of a gun? Even in my own neighborhood. Just the other day, my neighbor's house was burglarized. Last month, my car battery was stolen in broad daylight. My cousin's kid is hooked on drugs."

"He's right," added Oggie. "Do you know how much we could reduce prices if it weren't for the thefts and vandalism? People can't talk peace when they're just trying to survive. And we're talking the whole world here, Winnie. You always were a dreamer, buddy, and we love you for it. You're idealistic. That's refreshing, but peace on the scale you're talking about has never happened and never will. Jesus tried, and look what they did to him. If he couldn't do it, who are we?"

McEntire's voice was startling in its quiet intensity. He interrupted a brief silence with, "Last night a friend of my daughter's was raped in a parking lot. My daughter has been afraid to leave the house to visit her. The woman across the street is going to have her third abortion next week. I have to agree with Og. You've got to be more realistic, or the world will eat you alive."

"It can eat you alive in any case, so why not—"

Girardo interrupted Winston, "Winnie, we love your optimism, but I agree with Mac and Og, you're a dreamer. If you could hear what I hear every day in the pool hall...I've been robbed twice. One of my employees, the nicest woman you could meet, the customers love her...she was seriously injured in the last holdup. At least she survived. At the gas station and mini-mart down the street, the clerk was shot and killed in a robbery."

"And that's just here in this city. Multiply that by the whole world," Oggie said seriously. "I mean, we have the ability to vaporize the planet! We have enough nuclear warheads in this country alone to blow the Earth out of the universe many times over again. People are too afraid to talk peace. Peace is a rich man's cocktail topic."

An awkward silence followed Oggie's words. Tears came to Winston's eyes.

"Even while you argue against it, Oggie, I can hear the regret in your voice. Underneath the fear, we all believe it's possible. If we really believed the pain and violence was inevitable, it wouldn't hurt as much as it does. In our private thoughts, we say it: 'This is not the way it has to be. If only...if only what? If only someone had the courage to get the changes started? If only we would begin challenging the status quo? If only we allowed ourselves to really believe that it can change? We can! Dreamers have the answers. We should stop patronizing them and start listening to them.

"Maybe the dreamers in the past, Jesus, Gandhi, King, maybe they didn't bring about world peace, but maybe they started the process. Not everything happens all at once. Maybe we are just another step in the long process. Just because it may not happen tomorrow doesn't mean we're nuts to believe it can happen. But if we do nothing, it never will happen.

"Not too long ago, they called people nuts when they spoke of flying like the birds. A half century ago, the idea of putting a man on the moon was a fantasy. Today we have the world's knowledge at our fingertips. Who would have believed it forty years ago? The internet has brought the world to our doorsteps. Ask the right questions, find the right answers. Learn to believe, and then act, and anything is possible. Fear closes doors, love opens them. Let's start opening them instead. If we only achieve peace in our own souls, isn't it worth it? And maybe, just maybe, we'll be the generation to see it all come to pass. As Gandhi said, 'Be the change you want to see in the world.'"

"You're a dreamer, Winston, but you're a convincing dreamer," interrupted Ira with a shake of his head. "I guess since my bridge night has been cancelled, I could spare a night a month."

"You might as well count me in too," added Oggie.

"Who knows, maybe old cynics can learn new tricks, Oggie," teased Girardo. "Okay, Winnie, you can have the bar one night a month to plan the future of the world."

"Just a backroom would be enough, Girardo. We can join the patrons afterward and play pool."

"The backroom it is. Not too fancy for such a big purpose."

"If it were fancy, we'd just settle in and get comfortable. That's the last thing we need right now." McEntire's voice had been quiet so long, the others were a little startled. Winston noted the intensity in the man's voice.

"Does that mean you're in, Mackie?"

"You knew I would be."

"The Backroom Gang. I like it." Oggie smiled excitedly.

Winston tossed a shelled peanut into the air and tried to catch it in his mouth. He missed.

"You never do that, Winnie! Who wants a leader who can't catch a peanut in his mouth?" Oggie snatched the next peanut in flight and popped it into his mouth.

"I'm not your leader," said Winston. "Our paths just happen to be converging right now, and I could see it first. I'm no different. Except maybe that I'm an impractical dreamer."

The others chuckled.

"By the way, whatever happened to Craig?" Winston continued. "I have received so much as a Christmas card from him in years."

Ira twitched his finger to catch Winston's attention and answered coolly. "He became a writer of inspirational books and was developing quite a following. He moved to New York—"

"I remember that."

"His wife died," McEntire continued. "I heard he took to drinking after that. He came through town on his way to the mountains one summer. He said he was going to the mountains to write. I haven't heard from him since."

"None of us has," added Ira.

"He was everybody's best friend. I think he should be part of this group. Let's seek him out."

The others nodded in agreement.

"Can we bring other friends?" asked Oggie.

"If this is going to work, we all have to do what our hearts and our natures tell us to do. Sure, we can bring in others. I made a list of things I think we'll need for our meeting in September. Feel free to modify it as the spirit moves." Winston handed out the copies of his list. They all stood.

"This is insane," muttered Girardo with a smile.

"Yeah, isn't it great!" said McEntire with a bright, almost childlike smile. "Just like old times."

The old friends watched as Winston's jet lifted off the runway and swung to the west. Beyond the runway, somewhere over the city, a skywriter etched the sky in colored smoke. The message read simply, "I Love You." The men looked at each other.

"Don't ask," smiled Girardo.

DECLARATION OF THE WORLD

Winston arrived home late in the afternoon from a business meeting in the last week of August. He noticed an envelope from Antwerp waiting for him. Tired, he tossed it aside, poured himself a shot of brandy, and retired.

Awakening at five in the morning, his usual time, he read the letter from Michael in Antwerp. He reread the letter, thinking how great it would be if he and his son could work together toward their common goal of world peace. He thought of trying to call Michael, but instead he threw on a robe and went downstairs for breakfast.

Sandi was sitting at the kitchen table eating a blueberry muffin and drinking freshly squeezed orange juice. He circled behind her, put his arms around her shoulders, and kissed her on the top of her head.

"Good morning, handsome."

"Good morning yourself, you vision of loveliness."

"Vision of morning breath, more like it."

"Morning breath of fresh ocean air!"

"I don't believe a word of it but don't let that stop you. Flattery will get you at least a blueberry muffin."

Winston sat down next to the woman whom he still considered his best friend. They talked, laughed, and reminisced over breakfast.

At noon, they still had not dressed. Time disappeared for them, and their morning stretched into a week. They walked. They rode bikes. They picked flowers. They pulled weeds and became covered with mud and leaves. They selected old records and danced. They reveled in the intensity of the love that had lasted all those years.

September arrived like the bort from a diamond; everything was fragmented and gritty. The information that Winston and his friends gathered for their first meeting was the most primitive sort. How would they end up with the polished, priceless gem they envisioned? Still, they met, discussed direction and purpose, and labored on. In preparation for their larger work, they struggled to keep all of their personal actions and words as peaceful as possible.

Months passed. Their meetings were quiet affairs in the backroom of Girardo's club. Between them, they contacted communities all over the globe. They wrote about their observations. They read and wrote about what they read. They researched the constitutions of many countries, as well as the laws that resulted from those documents. They paid particular attention to peaceful areas of the world. Those who learned what they were doing called them dreamers, idealistic fools. Almost all shared their goal of peace, but few thought it possible to achieve in anything but a small area for a short time.

"Has anyone located Craig yet?" Winston asked. They were lounging in the backroom of Girardo's pool hall perusing papers and making notes.

"No. Just a rumor that he's been writing in the Lake Tahoe area," answered Ira before popping some peanuts into his mouth. "Oggie and I made a visit to his old neighborhood, and quite a few people offered their versions of his disappearance."

"One lady told me that he went off the deep end after his wife died. He started popping up all over Northern California, preaching to people about angels visiting him," added Oggie.

"He would go into bars and tell people to reach out for the Creator's wisdom," said Ira. "Great message. Weird location."

"They said the FBI was after him," continued Oggie with excitement in his voice. "Something about some letters to the United Nations."

"A neighbor with a friend in Tahoe said that Craig got into a boat one day, rowed out onto the lake, and just disappeared."

"Could he have drowned?" asked Girardo.

"Yes, except another neighbor claims to have seen a letter from him just a few weeks ago," explained Oggie.

"One of us should go there and try to locate him before our next meeting," said McEntire, sitting up.

"Good idea," added Girardo.

"Well, I have the time to do that but not the finances," said Oggie. "I'd be happy to volunteer if I could afford it."

Winston pulled a VISA card out of his wallet and tossed it to Oggie. "I'll take care of the financial end. Why don't you take your family and make a vacation of it, Oggie? I know I can trust you not to misuse the card."

Oggie rolled the card over, examining it. "You can trust me but finding him is no guarantee he'll join us. I'm not the speaker you are, Winnie, and everyone seems to think we're a bunch of crazy dreamers. All the money in the world isn't going to change that."

"Rainbow chasers, that's the one I heard yesterday," added McEntire.

"Oggie, the only difference between a dreamer and a visionary is time. People call you a dreamer until it comes true, and then they call you a visionary. Do you want to quit?" Winston looked at his friend with genuine empathy. "It's not easy being called a lunatic."

Ira leaned forward in his chair and said earnestly, "People I've talked to say they need leaders not dreamers, leaders who will work with the realities of the world."

"Which realities?"

"You know what they mean, Winnie," Girardo stood and began to pace. "Food and clothing and shelter, paying the rent, putting the kids through school. Catching a baseball game now and then. Making love."

"Those are all important, absolutely, and we can't ignore them, but what about hope and tenderness and the search for justice, equality, and unconditional love? Those things are just as real and just as universal. Why do they always get pushed to the bottom of the list when it comes to action?"

"It's hard to be just, when you're hungry, Winnie," signed Ira.

"Maybe if there were justice, there would be no room for hunger. It's not like the other approach has gotten us anywhere! There's no justice, and there's still hunger."

"People understand food better than they understand ideas," continued Ira.

"Maybe. But I think you underestimate people's ability to learn. If we have the courage to try peace, and peace brings prosperity, people will get the connection soon enough."

"Is there *anything* that can dampen your optimism, Winnie?" asked Ira with a mixture of exasperation and pride in his friend.

"Maybe, if peanuts became an endangered species." Smiled Winston, as he let a handful of the nuts roll from his hand into his mouth.

"But, Winnie, if the majority of us is satisfied with things the way they are, aren't we just hitting our heads against the wall?" asked McEntire sincerely.

"There's a difference between being satisfied and being afraid to change. I don't know anyone who is satisfied with the world the way it is. We can show them how to change."

"We're back to the leadership issue," Ira injected.

"Yes, and we have to be careful. The world doesn't need any more Hitlers or neocons that let power go to their heads," Girardo said soberly.

"We just have to remember that ideas count only if they are helping the people. Hitler was willing to sacrifice people to his ideas," answered Oggie. Others looked at him with mild surprise. "Hey, whatdaya think? I never have a deep thought?"

"I'm impressed," smiled Ira.

"If we stick to what's right, what creates good, how can we go wrong, no matter what the final outcome is?"

"Girardo's right," continued Oggie. "It's like that pledge that doctor's make: 'Do no harm' or something like that."

"I agree," concurred Winston. "Let's just hang in there and keep working for what we know is right. Keep acting on the truth."

The group silently focused back on the constitutions and other documents they had been studying. After a time, McEntire interrupted the quiet.

"What do we call what we're doing here?"

"Eating peanuts," answered Ira.

"What is this? Ira cracking jokes and Oggie being profound! What's the world coming to?" Laughed Girardo.

"Good things, Girardo, good things. If it can work with us, it can work anywhere."

"But, Winnie, what do we call what we're doing?" insisted McEntire.

"Eating peanuts."

Girardo hit Ira playfully on the head with the papers he was holding.

"Hey, you hit me! That's hardly peaceful."

"Yes," responded Girardo, "but how many people can say they've been beaned on the head by the constitution of a former Soviet state?"

"True, besides Gorbachev and Yeltsin."

"We can call what we're doing 'Peace at Last!'" said Oggie.

"Sounds too 60s," responded Girardo.

"How about 'Escaping Reality in the Hopes of a Better Illusion?'"

"Ira, you're such a cynic!"

"What are you, Girardo, the slogan police?" replied Ira.

"When you run a business, you have to know what's catchy and what gets the message across. I'd call it 'The Rebirth of the World.'"

McEntire gasped and put his hands to his face melodramatically. "Why, Miss Scarlet! I don't know nothin' 'bout birthin' no worlds!"

Oggie joined in again with "Freedom for All by Eliminating the Negatives."

"Too wordy," grimaced McEntire.

Winston interrupted their brainstorming patiently, "Our major concern is to try to make things more peaceful for this world through nonviolent means. I think the word 'world' should be a part of any label we give ourselves or our work."

"Peace in the World," interjected McEntire.

"Not bad, but…"

Ira jumped to his feet more excited than the others had seen him yet. "I know! I know! My friends, we here in this room are the composers of the 'Declaration of the World!'"

"That's it!" shouted Winston.

Like school kids who had just heard about their first field trip, they all began talking at once. Their paperwork was forgotten as they gravitated toward the pool table and began to play. In their excitement, they took chances and executed trick shots they would not have considered before. Ira began naming the balls after countries in the world that were at war or experiencing internal violence between factions, like Iraq in 2007. The men cheered each ball that fell into the "pockets of peace," as McEntire dubbed them.

After an evening of heady anticipation and certainty of success, the men returned to their daily lives. They had renewed energy when it came to applying the principles of peace in their own actions.

For a time, Winston was as excited and optimistic as the rest. In the middle of a study of various wars raging around the globe, however, he began to struggle with some serious doubts. Who were they, a ragtag group of pool buddies, to affect humanity on a global scale? Perhaps the cynics were right. Maybe they were just idealistic dreamers. Fools.

ARGUMENT WITH AN ANGEL

Winston's doubts led him into a state of mild depression. He went to bed earlier than usual and slept with certain heaviness. When the alarm went off in the morning, he crawled out of bed and put on his bathrobe. He wandered into his den and spied the papers he had left there the night before. He sighed deeply and flopped onto the couch. He closed his eyes and lapsed back into a fitful sleep.

Tavett appeared like a tiny mountain climber on Winston's shoulder. He took a deep breath and shouted, the sound of his voice reaching the man's ear more like the buzz of a fly than the call of a heavenly being.

"Winston! Winston!" he called, "Wake up! This is no time to sleep. Your work is going so well!"

The angel flew closer to Winston's face and tickled his ear, his miniaturized wings buzzing. He barely avoided the annoyed hand that swatted at the air. He fluttered over and blew lightly on the tender spot at the corner of one of the man's eyes. The sleeper groaned and scratched his eye.

"Winston!"

The angel grabbed a piece of hair that protruded from Winston's nose and yanked.

"Ow!"

Winston blinked awake and saw, through bleary eyes, the angel, now fully human sized, sitting across from him with a "Who me?" expression on his face.

"Go away!" Winston ordered. He closed his eyes again.

"Maybe I should have started with the bubblegum and yo-yo routine." Tavett offered.

"Go away."

"Why?"

"I'm through," said Winston.

"With what?"

"With you. With conditioning. With this whole lunatic thing!"

"Through with peace?" Tavett asked. "Through with justice? Through with love? Now, that's lunatic!"

"Fine. Put me in a straightjacket. Then go away."

"Miss Manners you're not."

"Listen, Tavett, or whoever you are, I'm exhausted," Winston explained. "I'm out of gas. I thought I could do this, and I was wrong. So just go find yourself some wannabe prophet. I'm a banker, not a priest."

"I detect some serious doubts here."

"Thank you, Sherlock. Now exit stage left, okay?"

"I don't think so."

"What? Heaven doesn't believe in freewill, in an individual's right to choose his path?" Winston asked.

"Of course heaven does."

"Good. I choose to sleep."

"And I choose to sit here. Just because I'm an angel doesn't mean I don't have rights too."

The silence lasted a minute or two.

"Quitter."

"Easy for you to say," Winston mumbled into a pillow. "You can fly out of here anytime you want. I'm stuck on this planet. Now, be quiet!"

Tavett sat for a little while studying the man on the couch. He stood and walked noiselessly back and forth across the room. Had Winston been watching, the angel's expression would have reminded him of his son when he was very young, standing in line for the restrooms at the state fair after drinking too many sodas. Exasperated, he finally spoke.

"You earthlings amaze me! You always think everything has to happen right away, and if it doesn't, something is wrong. You work yourself into a stupor over the lack of success you are convinced you will eventually have, even though it hasn't happened yet. You make an art form out of impatience! When someone has the nerve to suggest that you wait a little while for the results, you look at that person like you've just been kidnapped by aliens! You have no endurance! You have no persistence! You have absolutely no sense of history!"

Winston, resigned, groaned, and sat up. "What is this, your daily exercise in positive reinforcement?"

"What's to reinforce?" Tavett asked. "You're in your bathrobe whining about illusions of defeat!"

"And I'll have you know I know a lot about history. For instance, I know that the others who have worked for this cause—

Jesus, Gandhi, Kennedy, and King—and they've all ended up dead. I'd rather sleep."

"Of course, you would! Better spiritual suicide than the risk of actually acting on your beliefs!"

"Oh, get off your high horse!" snapped Winston. "What exactly have you done for world peace between flights to the cosmos?"

"You! You're what I've done!"

"Well, maybe you chose the wrong man. Beeep! Thank you for playing. Please pick up your consolation prize on the way out the door."

"I didn't choose you, mister!" replied Tavett indignantly. "I never thought you would be able to rise to the task. It was our Father who had faith enough in you to think you could do it."

"That's ironic, God having faith in me."

"What's so ironic?" the angel asked. "It happens all the time. Do you think his relationships are one-way streets? You don't know him very well, then."

"See, there's proof I'm not your man," Winton insisted. "Go find someone more worthy."

"Worthy? You think you were chosen because you're so great?" Tavett asked. "Brother! And I thought you had learned something!"

"I don't know what I think anymore," Winston said with a tone of exasperation. "I just know that I'm tired. I just want to spend time with my family, teach them to live in peace.

That's quite a job in itself, believe me."

"Yes, it is," the angel agreed. "And it could be enough if it were your path. A river must flow its natural course. Mountain lakes are fine, but without the rivers in between, the lowlands will die. A river can't spend its days pretending it's a lake. For some, settling in and lapping gently at the shores is true and good. For you, it is selfish."

"Why?"

"Because you're a river, Winston! It's what you are! Stop fighting it!"

"If this is my natural course, why does God let it hurt so much? Why am I afraid? This doesn't feel natural at all!"

"Because you keep looking at other people's paths as if they were options for you," Tavett explained. "You refuse to accept your way. Those who are stubborn and forget our Creator's natural order will always suffer tribulation. How can you not if you refuse to be true to yourself?"

"So that's what this is, heavenly tribulation?" Winston asked. "Thanks a lot!"

"I'm not doing anything to you. Neither is God. You are doing it to yourself by denying yourself."

"I didn't ask for this! I didn't plan this. I didn't even want it or even believe it until you came along."

"Aren't you listening to anything I'm saying?" Tavett questioned. "You are so pigheaded!"

"Some angel you are! Is name-calling part of your training in guardian angelship?"

"Only for those of us who have to guard stubborn, mule brained bankers," the angel replied. "Listen, Winston, this is not about who planned what. It's about learning to be who you are, to take the path that is a natural extension of you. It's about learning to flow your course to the sea. That's all."

Winston buried his face in his hands and began to sob. "I don't know how! I'm not strong enough! There has to be someone better for this. I can't handle it. I can't do it! I can't!"

"Let it flow, Winston. You see. Tears are natural. Let it flow," whispered the angel before lapsing into silence, waiting for the sobs to subside. As the man's crying slowed to airy sniffling, Tavett said, "Maybe you need some more tribulation."

"Oh, hey, great suggestion, Einstein. Then I won't be afraid."

"Seriously, Winston, this is good."

"What, my soggy sleeve?"

"Don't you see? You are realizing that you are only a man. You will be expected to do only what a man can do, what is in your nature—no more, no less. You're not some superhero. You are just, well, Winston."

"I'm not sure what that is. Sometimes I feel like an illusion."

"You will understand yourself better the more you accept your path and follow it," said Tavett. "You are not some messiah who has to take the burden of the whole world on his shoulders. People all over the world are being conditioned just like you are. Others have been in the past, and many will be in the future. You are a part of something that began long before your birth and will continue long after you are dead. Many of the enlightened ones have been just as reluctant as you are. And as stubborn."

"But how can just a few achieve something as big as world peace?"

"To those who believe, all things are possible," Tavett offered.

"Even if I believe, there Is so much opposition," complained Winston.

"People in the world who do not accept their paths become all tangled up and get in the way, that is true. That makes it difficult for everyone. Commitment to your true path is not easy. Commitment to a worthwhile cause is not easy. But listen to me," the angel continued in a tone of gentle authority, "you have already planted seeds. Many others are doing the same. You can't see the results yet, but when the garden grows? Beautiful!"

DREAM SPEECH

Winston had a dream a few nights after the argument with his guardian angel. He saw himself walking out of a sunny field and into a dark forest. The path he was following narrowed and the light dimmed. Brambles scratched his legs. He tried to turn back, but a large fly hovered in front of his face when he turned around. Off in the distance, outside of the dream, he heard a voice say, "Oh, real nice image, Winston." For reasons that made no sense in the dream, he chuckled. He continued down the narrow, uneven path.

After a time, he noticed the light begin to brighten. He pushed past a large branch and then a tall bookcase filled with pool cues and came out into a sunny meadow. On the far side, sitting on a large rock beside a clear stream, was Winston himself. He walked quietly over and sat at his own feet. The self on the rock began to speak.

"Why is wisdom so hard to find? It cannot be found in the classroom or dug up from the back of a closet. In fact, it cannot be found at all. It is lived. It is not in facts and figures, but in the application to all other things. Wisdom is in the connections. The high crossroads are reached through patience and practice. It is there always. It is available to any man, woman, or child who will act upon the natural abilities within. They will know they have found the path, for they will be reborn with new thoughts and new power to seek the next crossroad. Sometimes power comes by pain and sometimes by joy. Sometimes it comes by both.

"The seeker must be honest with the true self. Hiding from one's errors and faults and weaknesses accomplishes only inertia. Any fool can sit and pretend to be something he is not. That requires little resourcefulness. And it has little reward. He grows cold sitting there stationary on the ground. He covers himself with the blankets of education, material gain, sex, and political power. But the hard ground is still cold. No matter how many blankets he piles on, he cannot escape the chill as long as he remains sitting.

"Many who are blessed with intellect, talent, and charisma try walking for a time, but they refuse to admit their faults. They are like vines that grow into the eaves and entangle there and grow no higher. These vines of ego and vanity eventually choke themselves there beneath the eaves.

"When another looks at you with eyes of pity or scorn, turn and walk, head high, and do not look back. That person is judging you by his own place and path when he could be using that energy to walk his path. Pay him no mind. Perhaps he will see with clearer eyes one day. Perhaps he will get on with his own search.

"I have learned that people can change only if they want to change. No amount of pleading, threatening, cajoling, manipulating, or lecturing can cause one fraction of an inch of movement if a person does not want to move. Oh, we can create illusions of change in others through fear but running from a threat is not the same as hiking down a path. Once the threat is gone, there is no progress to be seen. No change.

"Movement that is not positive, whether out of fear of ignorance or anger or laziness, makes the heart heavy. Negativity feeds upon itself and gives birth to more negative movement. He who reacts rather than acts lives in pain.

"Pain is a warning, an alarm. It is not good in itself, but it helps us find the wounds that need attention. We can use it as an excuse to despair or a reason to hope. Pain can be our motivation to act.

"So many people keep their emotional pain hidden away in drawers and boxes and trunks of the soul. One's emotions should be spread out on the dining room table at least once a day. More often, if there's any hint of pain or distress. Like mediums reading tea leaves, we should examine them.

"No one sets out to create pain. Everyone means well at some level at some time. Most often we hurt each other unintentionally. We walk with our eyes closed out of fear and run into each other. That creates more fear, and we squeeze our eyelids tighter. Our interactions become negative. By nature we hate the negatives, but instead of opening our eyes, we learn to cast blame on those with whom we collide.

"Many children are raised by adults who are already well practiced in blame, and since children are such easy targets, they live with constant blame and shame, constant negatives. The adults see the pain they cause but justify it by calling it constructive criticism. 'If only the child straightened up, I could lighten up.' And so the child even gets blamed for the blame.

"A good parent listens without judgment and responds without blame. A good parent rewards honesty and open curiosity. A good parent spends energy trying to seek and impart truth rather than trying to manipulate. The fruits of truth are always good in the end, even if they may start out sour. Give them room to ripen. He who criticizes is the harvester of sour grapes.

"In business, I see employers trying to get the most out of their employees by using negatives. Deceptively, this may seem to work for a time, but it is only the harping that is creating the results, not any real change in the employee. Woe to the constant critic who turns his back! He will soon learn where all that negative energy has gotten him. Broken individuals break things.

"So few people are loyal these days. How can we be loyal to each other if we see each other as threats? If we would each accept our own path, our own responsibilities to maintain our own movement, we would stop feeling so threatened. We could stop blaming, stop trying to control others. What do another's footsteps have to do with my walking, except to signal that I have companions at times on the journey?

"A free society should be the coming together of independent souls in the spirit of compromise. Compromise by nature involves choice. That is why voting is the heart of a democracy. Governments should not be about control but about the opportunity to compromise for the common good, to discuss our varied ideas and needs, and to choose a course of action with each other in mind.

"The only way to sustain a democracy is to realize that the true reality is the actions that people themselves choose to take. Forcing others to act creates an illusion of progress that will always backfire in the end. Democracy is the best system man has yet devised to govern. It involves freewill and individual responsibility. It is built on what is real. It can be corrupted by those who would use its institutions as mere cardboard facades for hidden tyranny. If the few are being denied their free paths, then the system is a fake and will rot from the inside. Control is never freedom, whether you are the controller or the one controlled."

The Winston on the rock grew silent. The Winston at his feet bowed his head and began to pray.

"Gentle Creator, perhaps I am living in a dream world, but I believe that peace is possible. Why else would you have guided me to my own peace? Yes, it is out of love, but you love all of your children, not just me, and so my triumph over injustice and pain is a kind of model of what can be for everyone. Great Parent Who Loves Unconditionally, I believe you have conditioned me to help teach others the way to peace and the wisdom which sustains it.

"I believe that I am to love and cherish my family. I believe I am to help them grow. But I also have come to see that I have a family that is as vast as this world. How many others of every race, creed, and gender have struggled to rise about their own negative histories?

How many are still struggling now? How many despair of ever finding any rest?

"If I have found a measure of peace, how can I not give that back to the world that has been my place of seeking, my source of answers? In many ways, it is this world that has parented me, given me the space to look for truth and the tools to understand it.

"Father, you have helped me wobble onto my own legs and learn to walk. Please help me ease the pain in others by teaching them too how to stand. Thank you."

The sharp electric ring of the doorbell woke Winston. He groaned and rubbed his hand across his beard-stubbled face. Reaching for the robe beside his bed without opening his eyes, he remembered the dream of Winston's talk of people walking with eyes closed. He chuckled. His eyes stung as he opened them and tried to focus on the clock. It was nine in the morning, much later than he usually slept. The doorbell rang again. "I'm coming!" he whispered in exasperation.

"Registered letter, sir. I'll need your signature by the red x."

"Thanks."

"Sorry to wake you, sir."

"It shows?"

"Only a little, sir." Chuckled the delivery boy.

The return address on the envelope said South Lake Tahoe. Winston tried to recall who had mentioned Tahoe recently. He tore open the envelope and unfolded the letter, looking first at the signature. That's right, he remembered. Ira had mentioned that Craig might be in Lake Tahoe. He was right. The letter was from Craig.

Dearest Winnie,

How good it was to hear that you were looking for me! Oggie's not a bad sleuth. He tracked me down through a letter to the editor I wrote to one of the local papers about the pollution threat in the Tahoe basin. I want my great-grandchildren to see this lake as crystal clear as it is today outside my window.

I guess Oggie counted on the writer not being able to keep his pen still for long or his opinions to himself. Very perceptive! He said he was growing tired of reading every printed thing he saw. In his first week at the Lake, he's become an expert on local politics and culture. He even has his wife and kids searching papers, pamphlets, and books in their motel room. One of his sons said to me, "I'm glad Dad found you. I was beginning to feel like I was doing homework on vacation."

Oggie has a delightful family. Thank you for sending them my way. I suppose you are wondering what has become of me. No, Oggie and his brood did not find me in a drunken stupor in the parking lot of a casino. Of course, if they had come here a few years earlier, that would have been a distinct possibility.

After Gloria died, I thought I had no reason to live. I came here to be anonymous and drink away what was left of my life. But this place has a life force that just did not allow me to wither away. Eventually I began my own spiritual search. I'll give you the details when we meet. Suffice it to say that I began to become reconciled with death. That was followed by a deep desire to share with others a measure of peace that I found. I began writing books.

I was afraid that I was not ready to face notoriety should my books sell well (which they have, I am pleased to say). I needed the solitude of this beautiful lake's shores and ring of mountains to keep me on the path. I wrote under a pseudonym. A stronger man than I am could have been more open, but we must know ourselves if we are to find our way.

Perhaps you have read my work. I write under the name Sir Reginald Etchai-Veritay.

Winston paused, shaking his head. Sir Reginald Etchai-Veritay was a man whose writing had touched him strongly. And to think, it was his good buddy Craig!

Winnie, I am honored that The Backroom Gang wants me to join its efforts. I am excited about seeing all of you again, and I am even more excited about sharing the light. I will be at your next meeting to help compose the Declaration of the World. In the meantime, Oggie has given me a great deal of information about what you have done so far. I am humbled by the wisdom of the universe that has led us on such similar paths, though we have been apart. I trust this is as much a confirmation for you as it is for me.

In Peace,

Craig

THE GREAT HALL

The light turned the inside of his eyelids pink. He felt it waking him. "Will I never be able to wake to my alarm again?" He expected the angel's usual snappy answer, but none came. He fought the discomfort in his eyes as he forced them open. What he saw took his breath away.

There was a buttery golden glow around Tavett like a gilded aura. He was not dressed in his casual human garb. The robe he wore billowed in some silent, mystical, invisible breeze. At one moment it looked like gossamer white draperies, and the next it seemed to hold the dark star-scattered reaches of space.

It was Tavett but not as Winston had ever seen him. The angel's wings swept back from his shoulders like the sails of a clipper ship. They were huge, yet somehow not out of proportion. Tavett himself looked huge, though he fit easily into the room. The slightest movement of the white feathered wings sent the air rushing around the room, lifting papers off the dresser like a storm wind through an unsecured window.

The angel's face barely moved. It had a somber, yet comforting look. Colors swirled in his eyes like liquid opal.

"Tavett?"

"You have struggled with questions, searched for answers, and heeded your dreams. You have done well. You are ready for more, for movement to a higher plane: for visions."

"Why the—?"

"Where we are going I must approximate in physical form my spiritual self," Tavett interrupted. "It is a place of incisive honesty."

"Why now?"

"You were not previously ready, and it would have injured you. Visions are not for the tentative. Later than now would be past the time. It is the season now. Come. There will be time for questions."

The sweeping wings of the angel opened and stretched, and then with one swoop pulled the air, the angel, and Winston toward the ceiling. Winston cringed for the impact, which never came. He looked above and saw the depths of space. Behind him, he saw the earth shrinking and eventually disappearing. He saw planets and suns and asteroids. They passed a kind of veil, and he began to see objects and patterns of light for which he had no names. They rushed on. Direction lost all meaning, but there was a kind of comfort in the open vastness.

Suddenly Winston felt some pull akin to gravity, and the angel's wings wrapped protectively around the two of them. They began to spin slowly and descend feet first.

Winston's feet hit something solid. He felt a disappointment when Tavett's wings unfurled and left him standing independently. He was in a kind of great hall lined along the walls with thronelike chairs. Here and there in no particular pattern on the floor were tables filled with papers and books. Figures that looked like old men and women walked about, occasionally pausing at a table or to talk to another. A few sat on thrones sipping some drink and seeming to quietly contemplate. The constant murmur of voices, deep and earnest, vibrated in the air.

"Feel free to walk about." Tavett's voice seemed more formal. "Ask questions. Reap a fruitful harvest in your limited time here. Do not sit in the chairs along the wall. They are for the wise ones here to separate and meditate. Do not disturb those who are so engaged. They will hear you, and if they choose to join your search, they will do so. Those on the floor are engaged, and you may address them at your will, and they you."

"What is my purpose here?" Winston asked.

"Does your purpose change with your geography? What was your purpose yesterday or last week? Accept. Be. Seek. Give."

Winston gazed around the room. At times, the walls, floor, and ceiling seemed solid. At times, it seemed that the whole of the universe was contained in that room, and then that the room was the vastness of space and time, and then something beyond all space and time. He saw bookshelves and nebulae residing side by side in a most natural way. He stepped cautiously into the room and approached an old man bent over one of the tables. Or was it a planet?

"A man cannot turn the lawn green until he has learned to overcome the gravity that holds the water in the bottom of the well." It was the first thing that came to Winston's mind.

The old man turned sparkling eyes on Winston and answered him with a question, "In the life of your son, are you the pump which raises the water or are you the gravity that holds it down?"

"He must be his own pump. That I know," said Winston.

"Then you are the gravity." Puffed the old man.

"I don't exactly hinder him. I don't exactly help him."

"You are the gravity," the old man repeated.

"I am striving to water the grass in all circumstances, but I fail. I strive but make no progress."

Winston heard a dull thump and saw that a small black stone of some sort had thudded to the floor from space. Curious, he bent down to look and then picked up the stone. It was coal. He turned it over in his hand and grimaced at its plain, ugly surfaces.

"Can negatives be turned into positives?" he asked after he lost interest in the piece of coal. The old man quickly grabbed Winston's wrist with one hand and clasped his hand with the other, pressing the piece of coal hard against Winston's palm. He was strong for an old man, and the lump of coal hurt.

"Many a foot has been warmed by what you hold in your hand. And many a heart."

"Heart?" asked Winston. He opened his hand to look again at the coal, and there in his palm was a glimmering diamond. A second man, a distinguished-looking scholar, saw Winston's surprise and chuckled.

"Truth is too simple for us. We do not like those who unmask our illusions," said the scholar.

"You, you are Emerson, aren't you?" stammered Winston.

"Careful. He tends to believe his own pr."

"And you don't, Pascal?" retorted Emerson.

"Ah, you have me, Ralph," replied Pascal. He turned to Winston. "We owe a great debt to those who point out our faults for they humiliate us. They prepare us for the exercise of correction and freedom from fault."

"Most of my world does not want to see its faults," said Winston in response. "I was that way once too. I preferred my masks. I am in the process of stripping myself of the masks, facing myself with all my strengths and weaknesses, my good deeds and my errors. I believe that the world will have its illusions unmasked as well. It's inevitable. The time is approaching."

Winston expected some response from the two great thinkers. He had hoped they would affirm his comments. Instead, they nodded briefly and were gone. He saw Emerson, bending over a table on the far side of the room, and Pascal with his hand on another figure's shoulder, seemingly deep in conversation.

"What is true is simply recognized in this place. It needs no affirmation. That is an earthly insecurity which wishes to be told again and again that the same truth is true." Tavett was standing at his side.

"They will question what does not seem to fit until they dismiss it as falsehood or find room for it in their worlds by expanding their fields of vision. Ironically, these men who have eternity to ponder have no time for silly reassurances. They will not treat you as a student here, Winston. They will treat you as a fellow seeker, but they will answer any questions you pose. To learn, you must ask the questions. They will not preempt your search by assuming questions you do not ask, but they will be generous with their answers if you do ask. Move about. You can move like lightning here. Move. Ask. Take advantage of this window into the eternal." Winston looked across at a large cluster of spirit beings, marveling that they had once been limited to flesh and blood. He wished to be among them, and in an instant he was. He looked about at the kind faces and asked, "Is the freedom of peace possible in the world?"

Amiel turned to him. Winston was not sure how he knew it t was the spirit of Amiel, but he did. Certain things were simply true here and not necessary to question.

"To win true peace, a man needs to feel himself directed, pardoned, and sustained by a supreme power, to feel himself on the right road, at the point where God would have him be: in harmony with God and the universe. This reliance gives strength and calm."

An old Hindu priest whose name was hidden spoke, "The world is imprisoned by its own activity."

"Yes," agreed Augustine, raising one hand to punctuate his point, "but before God can deliver us from ourselves, we must undeceive ourselves."

"That is very true, my dear Augustine," added Emerson, who had joined the group. "Nothing can bring you peace but yourself. Nothing can bring you peace but the triumph of principles."

A Taoist monk entered the discussion quietly with, "If you are inwardly free of fighting, no one will be able to fight with you."

"Peace begins inside," mused Winston, "and lack of internal peace leads to external conflict."

"Yes," replied another voice, Fenelon. "It is only imperfection which complains of what is imperfect. The more perfect we are, the gentler and quieter we become toward the defects of others."

The spirit being, Bunyan, joined in. "Here a man shall be free from the noise and from the hurrying of Earth's life. Men have seen angels here."

"You mean in the place of inward peace?" asked Winston.

"Yes, I do."

"I understand," Winston exclaimed. "I asked, and now I understand. I feel the same excitement I felt as a kid when I started my quest."

"Let your understanding be your action," cautioned Kierkegaard.

Epictetus added, "No great thing is created suddenly, any more than a bunch of grapes or a fig. If you tell me you desire a fig, I answer you that there must be time. Let it first blossom, then bear fruit, and then ripen."

Winston felt satisfied that his question had been answered. He was about to tell the group so and thank them when he again found himself alone. The individual spirits had scattered around the room.

He looked up and saw stars and planets and wisps of colored vapors weaving in and out of them. He heard the murmurings of voices more ancient than his still earthbound mind could imagine, yet he felt a belonging more profound than any connection he had ever felt.

"I know that all of us are parts of a whole," he said to himself. "It is when we are truly ourselves that we can find unity with others, but in order to find ourselves, we must be free of ourselves, our egos that make us conform to something we are not in order to be admired or accepted. Nothing can deliver us from our false selves, except our principles, those that spring naturally from who we are. Yet too often when those principles prompt me to see my imperfections, I avoid dealing with them by being hostile toward others. I judge their faults to make myself look better in my own mind, and so accuse myself. I become a slave to my own faults. By not confronting them, I make them master.

"But there is always hope. Patience, persistence, and faith will eventually make a blossom that one day will bear fruit and ripen. If we have the will to see, we will eventually see. But how do I know if I am helping or hindering that process? How do I know if I am doing enough?"

"After a while comes the great awakening." The quiet voice of Chuang-tse startled him. Answers came so freely here, so quickly.

"We can give only what we have," continued Amiel, as if one in voice with the previous speaker.

"But what if I am not doing enough? What if I could do more?" asked Winston.

"To be wiser than other men is to be more honest than they, and strength of mind is only the courage to see and speak the truth." Hazlitt smiled patiently at Winston's doubtful look yet felt no obligation to convince him of the truth of his words. He simply spoke the truth and left the rest to the questioner. His faith in the final outcome of simply speaking the truth, his faith in Winston's ability to absorb that truth seemed a burden to Winston for a brief moment. Yet he marveled at the depth of respect he was being given by these beautiful souls of wisdom. It gave him courage to believe he could understand.

"You see, Winston," it was Emerson speaking. "The key to every man is his thought. Sturdy and defying though he looks, he has a helm which he obeys. He can be reformed only by showing him a new idea which commands his own."

"All that a man does outwardly," chimed in Channing, "is but the expression and completion of his inward thought. To work effectually, he must think clearly. To act nobly, he must think nobly. Intellectual force is a principal element of the soul's life and should be proposed by every man as the principal end of his being."

Winston felt a cool wind swirling around him, and he realized it was the breath of his own understanding. The others had left him to savor the clear air alone. The room became a meadow though it was still the room, also. He saw Plato sitting in his white robes on a low stone on the other side of the grassy clearing. He smiled at the Greek spirit as if at an old friend.

Plato smiled back and spoke, "Truth is the source of every good thing in heaven and on earth. He who expects to be blessed and fortunate in this world should be a partaker of truth."

"But truth can be dangerous," argued Winston. "Why do people ridicule, persecute, and sometimes even assassinate those who are working for truth and its children, justice, liberty, and peace?"

Schopenhauer leaned on a tree and replied casually, as if discussing the weather. "Mental superiority of any kind always tends to isolate its possessor. People run away from him out of pure hatred and say all manner of bad things about him by way of justifying their actions."

"Nevertheless," said Haydon, from his place on a stump, "never disregard what your enemies say. They may be severe, they may be prejudiced, they may be determined to see only in one direction, but still in that direction they see dearly. They do not speak all the truth, but they generally speak the truth from one point of view. So far as that goes, attend to them."

The patch of ground upon which Winston stood became a small sailing vessel, and the room a vast, limitless ocean canopied with a bright, blue, cloudless sky. Winston stood on the bow and watched the bowsprit bobbing and pointing toward the distant horizon.

"I don't possess any kind of superiority. I am weak so often, and I give in to habits I am trying to overcome. I believe in truth, but I doubt my ability to distinguish truth from lies. After all, others who are equally concerned about truth hold differing opinions because of their experiences. When I see the vast sea of things that are held to be true, it all seems so ludicrous. How can we know which is truth? What is the thread that makes life have meaning? What is the purpose by which we can judge an idea?"

Winston heard a rustle behind him. He looked over his shoulder and then turned in wonder. There on a raised portion of the deck sat Buddha, smiling. "The truth is the end and aim of all existence, and the worlds originate so that truth may come and dwell therein."

"So truth itself is the purpose? Truth is not a means to an end but the end in itself?" Buddha continued placidly, "Those who fail to aspire to truth have missed the purpose of life."

A man with a goatee and feathered cap appeared on the upper deck at the top of the ladder leading up to it. Winston recognized Shakespeare from drawings done of him. "Truth makes all things plain, Sir Winston."

"But is my truth really true?"

"There are more things in heaven and earth than are dreamt of in your philosophy."

"Then if truth is so vast, how can I know if I have even a piece of it? How is that possible, given the potential for error? How can I know?"

"I think," answered the bard, "that Sir Kempis there has as good an answer to that query as any."

Kempis stood at the rail on the starboard side. "Thank you, Master Shakespeare. It's easy, Winston. It's not just you. God is able to do more than man can understand."

Contemplating the answers of these new friends, Winston pulled himself up to sit on the railing of the boat. Instead he found himself sitting on a branch of an apple tree. The red fruit pulled the outer branches into sweeping arches that almost touched the ground. Beneath the tree, several spirits of the wise ones stood picking and eating apples. Winston smiled.

"You seem to be anticipating my questions. You must enjoy the curiosity of others as much as your own. I find myself wondering about results. If so many people are concerned and working for peace, why aren't they getting any results?"

Thoreau looked up at Winston. "There are thousands hacking at the branches of evil to one who is striking at the root."

"And it is that one who counts, Henry David."

"Don't mind his patronizing tone, Winston," said Thoreau with a smile. "Emerson here will always look on me as his protege."

"And a difficult one," teased Emerson. "You see, Winston, society never advances. It recedes as fast on one side as it gains on the other."

"Are you saying that growth must happen on a personal level? And peace?" asked Winston.

It was the spirit of Vivekananda who answered, "Whatever we are now is the result of our acts and thoughts in the past, and whatever we shall be in the future will be the result of what we think and do now. When it comes, the higher powers and possibilities of the soul are quickened, spiritual life is awakened, growth is animated."

"Each heart is a world," added Lavater, ducking out from behind a bending branch. "You will find all within yourself that you find without. The world that surrounds you is the magic glass of the world within you."

"And so it begins and ends with the individual, and the conditions of the world are the reflections of the conditions within. A family lives in peace when its members are at peace within. And a nation..." Winston mused.

Suddenly the apples began to fall from the tree like hail. As Winston watched fascinated, the apples rotted, the seeds sprung to life, and a thousand trees began to grow. He was lifted onto their branches toward the sky. A throne similar to the ones along the walls of the Great Room hovered in the sky. A Jewish man in traditional Middle Eastern clothing and a beard sat there. His eyes were kind and immensely strong. He spoke with gentle authority. "No man can serve two masters."

"Jesus?"

Winston suddenly found himself on the soft carpet of his den. He looked around, startled. Tavett sat there in jeans and a white shirt, his knees pulled up to his chest.

"What did Jesus mean? What other master am I in danger of serving?"

"What master should you serve?" Tavett questioned.

"Truth."

"And when have you felt discouraged in seeking truth?" the angel asked.

"When I feel the burden of changing the world," Winston answered.

"The outside world?"

"Yes."

"As if that is in your control?" Tavett asked.

"Pride," said Winston. "Pride is the other master, thinking that I am going to somehow change the world single-handedly. I am just one man in a long history of seekers. And my greatest responsibility is to embrace truth on the inside and live it in my actions. I can see now that history is my foundation and my comfort. I am a part of something larger."

"Follow your own path and leave the results to God and to time," Tavett advised. "Otherwise, you will grow impatient thinking that your actions are not changing things as they should. That will lead to either despair or arrogance. Both will hinder you."

"Thank you, Tavett. You have done so much to help me see."

"I too am following my path, Winston, but I am happy that your mission has been accomplished."

"What?"

"So far," the angel smiled. "Now go meet your friends."

THE SIGNING OF THE DECLARATION OF THE WORLD

"Of course, I didn't believe those silly rumors about your drowning in the lake!" protested Ira, as he wiped away the wetness on his cheeks. They had all greeted Craig as if he were a soldier returning from the war. In a sense, he was, but the war he recounted to them was one that had raged inside him: a battle against despair, self-doubt, anger, disappointment, and the alcohol that heightened the negative feelings.

"No, he just thought you had become a lunatic, writing mad ramblings on the top of a mountain!" taunted McEntire.

"That's not true! Perhaps a hopelessly addicted gambler haunting the casinos with a girlfriend wearing sequins and big blonde hair…"

"We are all very proud of you, Craig, for all you overcame," said Winston seriously. "And then you had the compassion to give back to the world that had hurt you by writing those books."

"I still can't believe I was reading your work this whole time!" marveled Girardo. "I should have known it was you."

"It was a different me than the one you knew well. I did a lot of searching and growing before I wrote those books," answered Craig.

"You must have done a lot of forgiving," said Oggie.

"If the world hurt me, it was out of its own pain and fear. Yeah, I had to forgive—the world and myself. I had to let the blame and anger go. That's why I'm here with you guys. I want to keep sharing the healing I've experienced."

"This has really been a healing time for all of us," added Ira. "The peace I feel inside sometimes still amazes me."

"Let's hope we can contribute to that peace being felt across the world," said Oggie.

"Shall we?" prompted Winston, gesturing openly with his hands. No one had to ask what he meant. The men nodded, reaching for their notes, and took their places expectantly around the long table that Girardo had set up in the middle of the pool room. All eyes turned to Winston, who remained standing at the head of the table.

Winston produced from his open jacket a gold pen. Holding it up like a shining baton, he began speaking with reverence. "Our work is finished, gentlemen. Let's put our signatures to it. This document is our offering to our fellow humans. Now our mission is to pass it on to whoever is willing to continue the race for peace."

Oggie accepted the pen and signed the document. As the others signed it, Winston continued, "Dear God, bless this our…"

Declaration of the World

It is the natural human condition to seek peace. Therefore, it is inevitable in the course of human events that it sometimes becomes necessary to recognize, disarm, and dissolve negative influences. In these times, every individual must focus upon the life-giving laws of nature, both in the world and inside the soul. In these times, every man, woman, and child must search for truth. In so doing, each individual shall recognize one's inalienable right to life, respect, love, liberty, and the pursuit of happiness, under the laws of nature.

Government is good when it serves as a bridge between the individual's liberty and that of the collective society of individuals. By definition, a good government recognizes the absolute equality, under law and custom, of all people regardless of any and all differences.

To secure the rights of all people under the immutable laws of nature, governments should be established by men and women of good will. When any government, whether by war or greed or land lust or lust for power or any other negative desire destructive to the human spirit, should cease to nurture the needs of the people, it is the right of the people to alter or abolish that government and institute a new government, laying as its foundation the happiness, freedom, and safety of every person living on the globe.

A government should not be terminated out of mere dissatisfaction, but rather in the face of actual abuse of the individual's natural rights, abuse which is intrinsic to that system and cannot be resolved within the established order. Should such abuse exist, for even the smallest minority, then it is the duty of all free and thinking men and women to find another way. Let the standard be the natural law by which all people have the right to choose a path to their dreams while respecting the paths others have chosen—in peace. Let all man made laws be based upon this law.

It is the inherent responsibility of all governments to seek to secure the rights and freedoms of all inhabitants of this globe and thereby secure peace for the nation which it governs. Such governments must continue to recognize the interconnectedness of all life upon the planet, and the need to consider the growth of all as beneficial to every group regardless of national borders.

It is a time of rebirth of human liberty, and that government which does not denounce narrow interests and embrace peace will not stand. That government which refuses to see war as obsolete will not stand. That government which makes of any individual or group a scapegoat for the struggles of another group will not stand. True government of the people, by the people, and for the people—all people without exception—will rise in the ashes of such governments and will unite all mankind under the natural laws of cooperative harmony, of peace.

Patience. Empathy. Action. Courage. Enlightened faith. Peace. These elements, which spell peace, are now in place and moving against all tyranny, whether personal, societal, or governmental. It is the unstoppable flow of history which now carries these into prominence. Liberty is a power which cannot be long suppressed. A government which seeks to bind the human spirit does so to its own peril.

We, the people of the world, in order to establish the means for our happiness and prosperity and that of our descendants do hereby serve notice that oppression on any scale, that temporary solution to yet unsolved problems, will no longer be tolerated. It has never served to do anything but create a fragile illusion of security. We will accept only those government actions which consider the wellbeing of all people essential to the well-being of any person. We hereby declare our loyal support to that government which sees the global context of our search for all things good.

We call upon our institutions—governments, religions, schools, families—to recognize the inviolate sanctity of each man, woman, and child, no matter how distantly connected to that institution of geography, culture, ethnicity, belief or any other element of individuality. We call upon our institutions to recognize diversity as a natural state of life on the planet, and peaceful harmony as the goal of all who so recognize this fact.

We hereby declare that the high bond of world peace and cooperation will be fulfilled and sustained only in an atmosphere of honesty with self and between neighbors and nations. We must look with objective eyes at the strengths of each nation and culture, and we must be willing to incorporate those strengths into our international guidelines for governance which encourages freedom.

We recognize and will remind any leaders in the political realm that any threat to the wellbeing of the whole planet, whether from internal or external forces, will surely prevail against us in our condition of fragmentation, distrust, and blame. It is therefore essential that we begin the process of converting our institutions to a more cooperative mode globally. In the prosperity of one lies the prosperity of all. We can no longer survive the division of ourselves in opposing camps. The era of provincial interests is gone forever.

As loyal citizens of our various families, groups, and nations, and as recognized citizens of the planet, we do commit ourselves and pledge ourselves in sacred bond to the pursuit of universal peace in which we and the world's children for all generations to come may prosper and grow on the paths which they choose for themselves.

The group said nothing when Winston finished reading. Each seemed absorbed in his own thoughts. After a period of silence, there was a sharp rap at the door.

"You guys ready for the cleanup in there?"

The men began to chuckle.

"We shall see," replied Winston.

"What?"

Winston began to realize that the real cleanup work—for peace— was just beginning.

THE RACE FOR PEACE: TRAINING

It was late in the evening. Winston sat at his desk in the den reviewing notes for his presentation to the governmental affairs committee of the United Nations and then to the United Nations General Assembly, and for his speech to the peace rally afterwards in Central Park. He heard Michael coming in from his date and smiled, momentarily remembering the way he used to screw up his face and say "Yuck!" when anyone talked of girls in a romantic way. Time passes.

He heard Michael's footsteps disappearing down the far hall. Before they faded, they stopped and then became louder. Michael was returning. A gentle knock on the den door signaled his arrival.

"Dad?"

"Yeah?"

"Can I come in?"

"For you, that's what my doors are for."

Michael squeezed in the door as if the light was in danger of leaking out into the hall and not returning. He closed the door after entering. He looked at the papers and photos spread out on the desk.

"You and your friends have been accomplishing a lot. Everyone is talking about the debate over your declaration."

"It's a good beginning. All good works take time. The times when there are no fireworks and media cameras are the most fruitful times. I spend so many hours in frivolous interviews lately. I wish there were some way to know which ones are going to be real opportunities to teach and which ones will be just fluff. I'm rambling. I'm sorry. I've been sitting here alone for hours."

"You must have gotten home just after I left."

"What's on your mind, son?"

"You were right about Jack and the college money," Michael confessed.

"What do you mean?"

"You shouldn't have given it to him. He just partied it away. He paid more attention to women than to his books. I'm sorry."

"Don't be. My reasons for refusing the money were not good. Besides, being generous is its own reward. We aren't responsible for what other people do with our generosity unless we know beforehand."

"I can't believe I trusted Jack," Michael admitted.

"Trust is not a bad thing, son. You aren't the one who fouled up. And don't judge Jack too harshly. He's a fine young man, and I suspect he'll learn from the experience. Once things get difficult, he'll think about how much better he could have spent the money. Then next time may be different. He has a lot going for him. I believe he will succeed. If his dreams are strong enough, and he's willing to sweat a little, he'll find his happily ever after. Let's pray he becomes a benefit to mankind."

"How can I trust him again?" asked Michael.

"Be cautious but be forgiving. Leave the doors open."

"I guess that makes sense."

"I have something for you, son."

"Dad, I have to tell you—"

"Here. Open it."

Michael sighed and opened the package. "A baton?"

"Like the ones the racers use. I'm passing it on to you."

"It?"

"My work. My businesses and the committees for peace."

"But, Dad—"

"Not all at once, of course, but I'd like to start by taking you to New York with me two months from now. You can watch your old man in action and get a feel for the work. In time, you can start working actively for peace through the businesses, through the peace networks we're setting up."

"Dad!"

"What?"

The Markovich Gallery has agreed to do a show of my work. It's a very important gallery. They have connections. The opening is the night before your speech."

"But what about our work?"

"Your work, Dad. My work will be hanging on the wall at the Markovich."

"Oh, I see."

"Dad, I love you, and I admire you. I'm very proud of the work you are doing, but it's not me. Can you see me trying to organize all the notes, actually speaking before some huge crowd in Central Park? I work at an easel. I paint my thoughts, draw my dreams. I connect with people in a different way. A quiet way. You're the one who taught me to march to my own drummer. How can I follow in your footsteps when I have my own to make? I believe in peace as strongly as you do, Dad. I just have a different way of making it."

"I don't understand your way," Winston said. "It seems so impractical."

"Sounds like what the critics said about your declaration."

"Touché."

"But you believed in it and put it out there. People read it, and it moved them. They translated it into all sorts of action that you could never have anticipated. That's how I feel about my art. Look at the painting I gave you last month. Why did you hang it up?"

Winston looked over at the painting hanging by the door. It showed multitudes of people ringing the earth and extending their hands in a gesture of peace. "I put it there to remind me of our—my goal of world peace every time I walked out this door."

"Our goal, Dad. The painting inspired you. Probably there have been days when you wanted to ignore your path, but that painting kept you focused. That's what I do, Dad. I connect with people in a private way, but it's just as powerful as speeches."

"I can see your point," Winston said.

They sat in silence for a moment.

"Dad?"

"Yes?"

"There's something else."

"What?"

"I'm getting married."

"Married…?

"She's pregnant, Dad."

Winston picked up the baton and slipped it into his jacket pocket. They stood, and he put his arm around Michael's shoulder. "Let's go get some sleep."

DR. JAN COOPER

THE RACE FOR PEACE: THE STARTING GUN

The next two months passed quickly. The nation as a whole was united as it had never been before without a declaration of war. The media dwelt on the possibility of world peace. The Backroom Gang had to sort through interview requests from every major media market. Already several nations had negotiated cease-fires in their conflicts, and others were investigating the possibility.

Academics and clerics and political leaders marveled at the unprecedented sweep of the New Peace Movement. Businesses began to seriously ponder the possibilities of open world markets. Each day saw the emergence of some new peace organization somewhere in the world. Rallies were being held in cities all over the planet.

Winston emerged from his speech to the United Nations under the glare of flashing cameras. World leaders jockeyed for positions near the man. He stepped to the podium bristling with microphones and held his hands to quiet the crowd that had spontaneously joined the press conference. He smiled, bent to the microphones, and simply said, "Peace!"

He could still hear the wild cheers of the crowd as the limousine turned a corner several blocks away. He would have preferred a taxi, but the mayor of New York City had insisted on the limo. He gazed out the window as they approached Central Park. The newly designed "peace flag" waved in a million incarnations along the streets. He closed his eyes to focus.

"Winston, let's go! The crowd is waiting!" Oggie's big smile was the first thing he saw when he opened his eyes. He could hear the chanting of the crowd.

"PeaceForeverPeaceForeverPeaceForever."

The sound rose and fell like waves. Winston rode the waves to the stage. A deafening cheer rose from the grassy lawns of the park like a tsunami of sound. Winston and his pool hall buddies stood in awe. They could not even hear each other talk.

Near the front of the crowd, an artist's eyes filled with tears of pride. Unbeknownst to Winston, Michael had changed the date of his opening so that he could be in New York for the speech.

Winston stepped to the podium. The sound grew to a fierce crescendo. He smiled and raised his hands to signal silence. In a moment, such a hush fell that those on stage could hear a bird somewhere far back in the trees. The anticipation was electric.

"I am not here to start a new religion. I am not here to start a new country. I am not here to rise to some position of power. I am here to talk to you. I am here not to talk to you about something new, but rather about something as ancient as a newborn baby's first cry and a mother's comforting breast. I am here to talk to you of peace."

A roaring cheer rose and then fell. Winston continued.

"I will not presume to teach you about peace. Each and every one of you, my friends, knows peace. It is as much a part of you as the breath that sustains you and the water that courses through your veins. You need only look inside to your dearest dreams, to your fondest hopes for the future, to your most sincere wishes for your loved ones. What do you see there? Peace!"

"Peace!" shouted back the crowd.

"What do you cherish there?"

"Peace!" cried a million voices.

"What comforts you there?"

"Peace!"

"What will endure there?"

"Peace!"

"What will you release from there into a world crying for a better way?"

"Peace! Peace! Peace!"

Winston joined the chant and then raised his hand for quiet.

"Your voices are like music to me. It is your voices that will break the silence of fear and misunderstanding and prejudice and xenophobia. It is your voices that will engrave peace on the hearts of the world powers. Use your voices. Use them in your homes. Use them in your workplaces. Use them on the streets. Use them in your houses of worship. Speak. Speak in love about peace!"

When the cheering subsided, he continued. "But do not just use your voices. Use your hands. Use your hands in the soup kitchens. Use your hands at the sickbeds. Use your hands on the crying child's cheek. Use your hands at the voting machines.

"My friends, those of you who live in a democracy have a valuable opportunity. You have the right and the privilege to choose who will make the decisions in your government. Use that power. In the next American election, let us make history by the number of votes cast. If you are registered, vote. If you are not registered, be sure to register in time, and then vote. Use your copy of the Declaration of the World as your voter's guide. Use your hand at the voting machine to say to politicians, "If you do not govern for peace, you will not govern at all!

"If you do not live in a democracy, you still have the power of peace. In one way or another, all leaders govern by the consent of the people. Sometimes the consent is active, sometimes it is passive. If your leaders do not agree to govern for peace and you have no vote with your hands, then vote with your bottoms. Yes, your bottoms. Just simply sit down. How can a ruler rule a nation of sitters? If they will not stand for peace, then you sit down for peace. Move again only when they are moved. Take the power. Yes, there is risk. Yes, it will take courage. But we are with you. Show them, my friends. Let us all sit."

With a rumble of movement, the crowd throughout the park sat down.

"So that peace may stand!"

The crowd jumped to its feet cheering. Eventually, Winston continued.

"Peace begins at home. The United States is my country, and I love it dearly. It has not always stood for peace, but the past is the past. If I focus my energies here, it is because this is my home. I would like to see this country rise to the challenge before it as it has done in earlier times. If we can begin this reformation on ourselves, if we can overcome our fears, we can again be a shining beacon to the world, an example to be admired and emulated. America, embrace peace!

"We must elect forward-looking men and women who are committed to moving into an era of peace. We must elect innovative thinkers and courageous movers. But we must also elect men and women with keen ears to hear the dreams and ideas of an entire nation longing for peace. We must elect leaders who will hear us. Leaders who will hear the tired young mother. Leaders who will hear the frustrated high school student. Leaders who will hear the homeless father. Leaders who will hear the age tempered farmer. Leaders who will hear the silent whisper of the artist—"

Winston caught the gleam of a familiar eye in the crowd. He paused a moment. Father and son exchanged a look of understanding more profound than any words. The crowd stood still, expectant.

Two shots cracked the silence. An instant of confused paralysis gripped the crowd. A son's mouth opened in a silent scream. Winston stood on the border of consciousness as the blood began to drip onto his forehead.

"I'm getting better at around-the-world," the angel said smiling.

"I see you found some gum. Don't try blowing bubbles, okay?"

"Like the jeans? I wore them in your honor. They're—"

"I know. They're what I expect."

"It's time to go now, you know."

"Another visit to the Great Hall?"

"Yeah. A long one."

"What if I say no?"

"Are you going to make this difficult, Winston?"

"No."

"No, you won't make it difficult, or no, you won't come?"

"Some angel you are.",

"Can I take a last peek at my kid before I go?"

"Sure. He's a great kid."

"I know."

Michael wiped the tears from his vision frantically when he saw his father's eyes opening. He held his dad's head in the crook of his arm as he tried futilely to stem the flow of blood. He tried to fight the sobs.

Glancing toward the front of the stage, Winston groaned, "Tell them that…"

"Dad, I love you."

"You're a good son. The Lord will deliver you from all your fears. You're the best. You must always pray and never give up. Teach the young to serve the Lord. I love you kid. Teach people to live by faith not love. Now go to them. Paint them a picture, draw their names, give your workshops on *health, wealth,* and *miracles.* I see Jesus! He is coming in the clouds! Share Jesus! Share Jesus!" He smiled a pained smile and died. Michael dropped to his knees saying the Lord's Prayer. "Our Father whom art in heaven, hallowed be thine name. Thy kingdom come, thy will be done. On earth as it is in heaven."

A powerful wind, like the sweep of some hidden, giant wings, rushed upward from the stage. Winston's bloody coat fell open, and a small baton rolled out of the pocket. Michael picked it up reverently and smiled through his tears.

"Thanks, Dad."

Michael became aware of the unearthly wail that had begun in the crowd and continued like siren. He stood and gazed out at the people. Cameras flashed unrelentingly. The masses had begun an eerie sort of mourning dance. Heads rolled back. Arms shook fists at the sky. Hands pulled at hair. Bodies embraced in a futile effort to find comfort. The sounds of grief multiplied, rose, and fell. From far back in the crowd, an angry voice rose about the rest and shouted, *"No!"*

Michael could feel the anger begin to spread, pulsate. He had to move. He gripped the baton and stepped to the microphone.

"My name is Michael, Winston's son."

He waited as the sounds became a kind of inarticulate questioning.

"My name is Michael. I am Winston's son."

A desperate silence overtook the crowd. They were grasping for any thread of sense thrown their way. Michael was determined that these beautiful men and women, this living mural of a crowd that stood tribute to his father's faith, would not be left to drown in grief or resort to anger. With power in his voice, he continued.

"I am Winston's son, Michael. I stand here before you, baptized in my father's blood. As are you. As are we all."

A wail rose from the crowd. Michael held up the baton. "This baton…"

The crowd listened, curious.

"This baton is my father's gift to me. He knew he would be dropping out of the race. His lap is done. I pledge to you today that I will take this runner's baton and run to the finish line! Give me some time to mourn. Give yourselves some time to mourn, and then promise me that you will meet me back here, and together we will run the good race!"

Sirens faded in from the distance, echoing off the steel and concrete canyon walls of New York City. The crowd continued standing in silence.

"If my father could speak, I know what he would say to you at this moment."

He paused.

"He would say one thing only."

He paused again.

"Peace!"

The word seemed to stun the crowd. It hit like a spark and ignited. As the sirens grew louder, the bloodied son led the bruised crowd in the only tribute worthy of the man who lay dead behind him.

"Peace!"

"Peace!"

"Peace!"

"Peace!"

In languages as varied as the flowers, around the globe, the chant rose up before the television screens in town halls, before radios in dusty village squares. It spread out like the waves from a pebble skipping across a clear lake.

"Peace!"

"Peace!"

"Peace!"

"Peace!"

THE RUN TOWARD THE FINISH LINE

Michael rubbed his eyes wearily. He jumped when he heard the voice.

"I hear you're being hung in a rather prestigious gallery tomorrow. You should get your sleep."

"I suppose."

"Both great works, 'The Uniting' and 'World Peace,' hung on the walls of the chambers of the General Assembly of the United Nations. Pretty heady stuff. Your father is proud."

"Who are you?" Michael studied the figure clad in jeans and popping bubblegum. "How did you get in here?"

"Through your open door."

"I swear if that kid doesn't learn to lock a door . . ."

"You should be teaching him to unlock doors. Like your father did you."

"Who are you?"

"Your guardian angel. All people who believe have guardian angels."

"With jeans and bubblegum? Yeah, right!"

"Would you prefer wings and a white robe?"

"Please! You're lunatic enough just like you are."

"Déjà vu!"

"What?"

"Nothing. Just something your father said to me once."

"You knew my father?"

"Yup. Still do."

"How?" Michael asked suspiciously.

"I'm an angel. I get around. You are one of God's representatives here on earth. You have been anointed by the Holy One. You will aid people in healing and give them hope. God's word is like medicine."

"This is not funny. You're playing with some very tender spots here, fella. I don't know who you are, but I don't appreciate you barging into my house and making light of my loss." Michael reached for his cell phone and began to punch in 911.

The stranger's next words hit him somewhere between the first and second number one. "Be cautious but be forgiving. Leave the doors open."

"What did you say?" asked Michael as he snapped his cell phone shut.

"I said what your father said when you were so mad at your college buddy, Jack. Be cautious but be forgiving. Leave the doors open."

"How did you know about that?"

"I—"

"I know, you're an angel!"

"Is that so strange a possibility? I didn't mean to make light of your loss. It's just that your father and I used to joke in tense moments, and you reminded me of him and—"

"You still haven't told me how you know my father."

"I was his guardian angel. Now, God has chosen you. You will overcome evil with good and teach others to overcome temptation and make the devil flee. The goodness of God leads people to repentance. You have always been waiting on God and waiting on His timing."

"I try to keep up with the slang. Did I use that wrong?"

"Not really. It's just...Jeez, I'm talking to you like you're really here!"

"I am. How else could I have known about that comment your father made that night you snuck into his den to tell him your girl was pregnant?"

"Nobody knows that."

"I know. I won't spill the beans. By the way, your dad was right about Jack. He pulled it together after that first semester in college. He's leading peace rallies in Africa somewhere. He travels a lot. He became a doctor. You should call him. I could get a number."

Michael sat down with his mouth open. It took him a minute to speak, and then he did so with tentative belief.

"How's Dad?"

"Still driving the great philosophers crazy with questions. That is why I decided to come back here. I mean, I love him and all. But that man sure can talk."

"God has granted you a spirit of *wisdom*. Your spirit of loving Jesus comes as a result of His loving you first. Let the people know the Lord forgives all their sins and heals all diseases. He heals broken hearts and the sheep will hear God's voice. Trust me."

"What's the Great Hall?"

"I'll take you there someday. Man, we've got a lot to talk about!"

Michael looked toward Heaven with tears in his eyes saying: Dad the last words you spoke to me were paint them a picture, draw their names, give your workshops, and share Jesus. Oh holy spirit, help me! Help me! Help me to speak the right words and let all nations know that Jesus is coming soon! He is coming like a thief in the night! He is coming in the clouds! I see Him. I see Him coming too!

MIRACLES ARE COMING YOUR WAY

By Dr. Jan Cooper

Our Father whom art in Heaven, hallowed be thy name. Thy Kingdom come, Thy will be done on Earth as in Heaven. God has big plans for you. They are plans of good, not EVIL. Prepare for your transformation and our Savior's soon return!

It is time to become the STAR God wanted you to be in the first place. It is time to get rid of the RATS in your life. The rats are anything negative that is keeping you from your DREAM! Spell RATS backwards and you will become the STAR God intended in the first place.

The EVIL one wants you to have ANGER issues, but take the R off of anger and ad an L, SO YOUR angel can take over. For if you don't, put a D in front of anger and that is when DANGER takes place. The EVIL one wants you filled with ANGER and DANGER, so you can't fulfill the plans God has for you. But spell EVIL backwards. It spells LIVE. Once you get the EVIL out of your life, you will LIVE and have a happy prosperous life, the way God intended in the first place.

The HOLY SPIRIT will know, way before us, the direction and speed of when Jesus will return. That is why we need to get rid of the SPAM in our lives. Spell SPAM backwards then we will have the MAPS to help us prepare for when Jesus returns.

The EVIL one wants you to have lived so you cannot spread the GOOD NEWS. He wants you to have cancer, diabetes, heart attack, stroke, and self-doubt. He wants you to have LIVED so you cannot spread the GOOD NEWS. This is why it is very important to KEEP our faith. Spell KEEP backwards then we can PEEK into the future God has planned for each and every one of us.

Spell LIVED backwards. It spells the DEVIL. The DEVIL wants the worst for you. He wants you so STRESSED you will pray to die. But spell stressed backwards and it spells DESSERTS. God wants you to partake of the DESSERTS of life. He wants you to prosper. Miracles are coming your way. Be prepared to keep your faith. If you do NOW what you are supposed to and spell NOW backwards, then you have WON!

Miracles are coming your way! YOU WILL BECOME THE STAR GOD INTENDED IN THE FIRST PLACE! Be prepared to prosper so you can help others to prepare for HIS soon return!

TESTIMONY

You Become What You Think

There are many kinds of birds and people and they share some common characteristics.

The EAGLE is a bird of perseverance, strength, and determination. I relate to an EAGLE, and at the age of 82, have the courage to share my story. The EAGLE at the age of 40 has a major decision to make. It will fly to the highest mountain top and pluck out its chest feathers to grow new, sharpen its beak or grow a new one, sharpen its talons or grow a new one, or die. People are much like the EAGLE. At the age of 40 they too will change their eating habits and life or they too will die.

CHICKENS are usually afraid of life. They are lazy and live in the confines of a fence and are satisfied to do so. Many Christians are like CHICKENS. When storms or troubles hit, they run away and hide. When I was a young boy, I was like a chicken. I had no heroes, no one to believe in. I wanted to be like superman so I would not have to hurt so much. I was labeled a slow learner and put in remedial classes. At about the age of 16, I got on my knees and said, "Lord I am not sure if you are real or not but if you are, will you please make me good at something so I do not have to feel so dumb and stupid?" Ever since that time I have had a daily conversation with God.

MAGPIES are aggressive and abuse other birds. Many people and Christians do the same without knowing it. My mother once said, "Why can't you be like other kids?" She once held a toy gun to my head and said, "If this was real I would kill you." Others in the family always called me a dumb shit. All I remember about my youth is yelling, hollering, screaming and fighting. I was constantly told no good deed goes unpunished. My mother didn't believe in God. My dad's brother was a preacher and he came down with cancer. My dad always told his brother if he had led a good life like him he wouldn't be so sick. MAGPIE Christians don't believe in God and make fun of him. I knew I didn't want to become a MAGPIE and prayed to God to use me however He wants. Please make me good at something so I do not feel so dumb and stupid.

The KOOKABURRY bird his life is like one big party. When I was a young teenager I could stay out until 1:00A.M., and beat my parents' home. KOOKABURRY Christians do not take things seriously. Often they wound, hurt and offend others. Upon coming home late at night all my parents did was yell, scream, holler and fight. KOOKABURRY Christians have in most cases no idea they are hurting or offending people. Once I was attending my grandmother's funeral and my mother was picking me up at the airport. She said, "Do you miss my things?" She said, "Don't go to the funeral, stay at home with me." I too have hurt people without knowing it. I had no idea I was hurting my kids when I let them be adopted.

The VULTURE is the garbage collector of birds. I remember how my mother took a butcher knife and sliced my dad between the forefinger and thumb and my dad knocked her to the ground to protect himself. For some reason every time there was a robbery or bad happening in the news, I thought it was my fault. VULTURE Christians are drawn to people with problems and they use their words to destroy and love to see people suffer. Lord, help me to get rid of my problems. Please make me good at something so I do not feel so dumb and stupid.

The PARROT is a talker. Christian PARROTS are talkers who do not do the walk. I saw myself starting to mirror my parents. I did not want to be like them. Lord, please help me. I started reading the

Bible more, taking classes, attending workshops and discovering the kind of people I wanted to be like. I wanted to be like Dr. Norman Vincent Peale, Robert Schueller, Billy Grahm, Dr. Mike Murdock, Joyce Meyer, and Joel Osteen and many others. I forgave my parents for I realized they did the best they could they just did not know how to give what I needed. Just as I did not know how to give my kids what they needed when I let them be adopted. We now have been reunited for about 30 years.

PEACOCKS are beautiful and flashy. I married and divorced in my 20's. My wife today married the first time when she was16, I met her when she was 21 with two kids. They were four and one. When I was 31, I met my PEACOCK, she was so beautiful. I was awe struck. We all have been together for over 40 plus years and the four of us were baptized at Capital Christian center on Howe Ave back in the late 70's or early 80's.

PELICANS have big mouths and appetites. I had a big appetite to learn as much as I could so I wouldn't feel so dumb and stupid. By filling my mind with the LOVE OF GOD, patience, and persistence, I was a teacher by the time I was 21 or 22. I have always worked more than one job. I not only taught during the day but I taught night classes. I also was taking classes in the evenings.

The CANARY spends much of its time trapped in a cage. I never wanted to be mediocre and trapped into negative thinking. Jesus said I can do all things through Him. Because I believed him I have hosted my own TV Show, had a radio show, became a Graduate Gemologist, and was a teacher for 38 years. I, also, have become an artist, author, and speaker. I also quit smoking.

The CROW is cunning, dangerous, and only out for itself. Nothing matters but their own selfish desires. The CROW Christian enjoys hurting others, dividing churches, and ruining people's reputations. Many years ago a pastor has been to my home for dinner and I to his home for dinner. I started sharing with him some of my writings and he said I am the DEVIL He scared me so much I stayed away from church for years. Lord, I have seen too much of this in the name of religion. Help me Lord to bring people to you with the eye of an OWL and EAGLE not a crow.

An OWL represents WISDOM. I pray to have the wisdom of Moses. I pray to have the wisdom of David and Solomon. I pray to have the WISDOM and LOVE of Jesus. I pray to have the eye of an EAGLE and fly above the storms of life so the HOLY SPIRIT can take over.

The HOLY SPIRIT lets you know that Gods word spoken out of your mouth produces powerful victories. Now, I know the Lord saves His anointed. I have been anointed by the Holy One and so have you. I am called to anoint many who are sick and heal them. I no longer try to be popular with people. All I want to do is the will of God. I cry out to the Lord and he heals me, The Lord declares He will restore your health and heal your wounds. I am one of His sheep and the sheep hear His voice. When I walk in Love God is present. May you all be healed. God sent a Son and left us a book. Share your story it will heal you and those who need to read it. May you all be healed. JESUS IS COMING SOON! Please tell us your story. God loves you.

ABOUT THE AUTHOR

Dr. Jan Cooper has degrees in Speech, Drama, and Art. His advanced degrees include a master's degree in education from Oregon State University, and a PhD from The American Institute of Holistic Theology. Dr. Cooper has taught Art to troubled inner city youth. Some of his students have won scholarships to Disney Studios and a fashion design school.

Back in the 80s, Jan hosted his own tv show interviewing artists and authors. For a couple of years, he was a ventriloquist on a children's tv show. He also is a graduate gemologist and jewelry designer from the Gemological Institute in Santa Monica.

His most prestigious award and honor is the George Washington Honor Medal from the Freedom Foundation in Valley Forge.

He now writes daily from his office in his home.

www.ingramcontent.com/pod-product-compliance
Lightning Source LLC
Chambersburg PA
CBHW030556080526
44585CB00012B/391